THE FEAST ~OF THE~ OLIVE

COOKING *with* OLIVES *AND* OLIVE OIL

by MAGGIE BLYTH KLEIN

Illustrated by Mary Rich

CHRONICLE BOOKS
SAN FRANCISCO

The Noblest Olive of Them All, by L. R. Shannon reprinted from *The New York Times*, January 9, 1980. Living Section. Copyright © 1980 by The New York Times Company. Reprinted by permission.

Library of Congress Cataloging-in-Publication Data
Klein, Maggie Blyth, 1947–
  Feast of the olive : cooking with olives and olive oil / by Maggie Blyth Klein ; illustrations by Mary Rich. – [New and updated ed.]
    p.   cm.
  Includes index.
  ISBN 0-8118-0523-9 (pbk.)
  1. Cookery (Olives)   2. Cookery (Olive oil):   I. Title.
  TX813.04K56   1994
  641.6'463–dc20   93-38082
                                                            CIP

Printed in the United States of America.
Designed by Laura Lovett.
Typeset by Words & Deeds.

Distributed in Canada by Raincoast Books,
112 East Third Ave., Vancouver, B.C. V5T 1C8

10 9 8 7 6 5 4 3 2 1

Chronicle Books
275 Fifth Street
San Francisco, CA 94103

FOR ROB

CONTENTS

RECIPES 63

ACKNOWLEDGMENTS

My heartfelt thanks to my friends in Tuscany, Lorenza de' Medici and Piero Stucchi-Prinetti, for their generous and warm hospitality. Thanks also to Maurizio Castelli for his teachings, and to Virginia Nicholls for her trailblazing. Particular thanks to John Meis for withholding nothing—neither congeniality, nor anecdotes, nor marvelous meals.

My gratitude to Marion Blyth, Frank and Mary Robertson, Charles Perry, Nancy Friedman, and Eugenio Pozzolini for making available the results of their research.

Thanks to Pat Darrow, Anzonini del Puerto, Julie Smith, Peggy Anne Davis, Isaac Cronin, and Ann Walker for contributing their wonderful recipes.

My warmest thanks to L. John Harris, who conceived the idea for a book on olives and olive oil, and whose contributions—culinary, aesthetic, and editorial—helped give shape to the book.

Thanks to Don Blyth who proofread the original manuscript. And eternal indebtedness to the indomitable Rob Klein, and to my wonderful parents and brother, Richard Blyth.

INTRODUCTION

Since the first edition of this book in 1983, olive oil has become the "ubiqui-tous comestible" for many more Americans than it had been previously. Folks are now willing to pay extra for what they think of as fine olive oil; it is widely recognized as the most salubrious of oils. And even those exotic olives—Niçoises, Sicilians, Picholines—are appearing more and more on home antipasto plates along with such suitable companions as goat cheese and pick-led hot peppers.

My personal experience with olive-oil cookery has expanded as well, for in 1986 my husband and I opened Oliveto ("olive grove" in Italian) Cafe and Restaurant. The restaurant seems to have found a place in the hearts and pal-ates of lovers of northern Mediterranean cuisine, a table characterized by a few common flavors such as garlic and rosemary and by the use of olive oil as the main cooking medium. The chef at Oliveto purchases no fewer than eight different olive oils: a sweet, fruity oil for diners to dip their *focaccia* into at the table, a peppery Tuscan oil with which to finish risottos and grilled meats, a soft oil for dressing a salad of flavorful organic greens, a tasty but indestruc-tible oil in which to sauté garlic, a rough-hewn oil for marinating our lovely olives in, and so on.

That Oliveto Restaurant exists makes it possible for me to obtain the aid of a magnificent kitchen staff—chef, sous chef, cooks, and pastry chef—for help with certain recipes that, in the previous edition of this book, were "perfected" in a home kitchen and tested only by my friends, however expert they might be. At Oliveto, months and months of constant experimentation and sampling have yielded what we consider the best recipes for such essential northern Mediterranean (especially Italian) constituents as cannellini beans, polenta, and pizza dough. Not a modest claim.

I was born in California. Special dinners at my family's house always included a dish of green and so-called black-ripe California olives. I would steal both kinds from the dining room table as the setting sun filled the room and my mother was upstairs getting dressed for company. My rearrangement of the olives was a perfect cover-up for the theft, I'm sure. I wonder if, at that age, I would have loved shriveled Moroccan olives or cracked Sicilians as much. But I was in Los Angeles, not in the Lozère.

And ever since I began to cook, my taste preferences have been Medi-terranean. I never craved sushi or gravlax, although I liked them just fine. No doubt my mother thought I would give up my aberrant liking of olive oil.

Instead, here's a book called *The Feast of the Olive*. Mother can still take or leave olive oil.

If the cuisine of the Mediterranean could be characterized by any one flavor—one element that would change it utterly were it never to have existed—that flavor would have to be olive oil. Without it, the Berber shepherd, the gypsy in Andalusia, the housewife in Provence, the Tuscan vintner, the fishmonger in Calabria would never have been able to enjoy the wonderful meals they and their ancestors have been eating for centuries. Food prepared with the singular, fruity, and glorious taste of a good olive oil, accompanied by its old companion, garlic, is enough to transport anyone to some sunny clime close by the Mediterranean.

The importance of olives and their oil is not merely gastronomic. Olive oil has represented holiness, healthfulness, and plenty and has illuminated temples and homes for thousands of years. It comes from the most noble of trees, and from the most ignoble of fruits. It is astonishing that the ancients, with their limited knowledge of machinery and technology, discovered not only how to extract the oil from such a bitter and unpromising source, but also how to do so without damaging or adulterating the delicious liquid.

An ever-growing array of handsome bottles and cans of olive oil is filling our stores. Can we cooks who are anxious to create the flavors of the Mediterranean expect to find among them oils that compare with or surpass the quality of the oils made for Mediterranean cooks long ago? With a little knowledge, we can. It is unfortunate that the simple methods that produce the purest, least modified olive oils are being replaced more and more by industrial processes. Consequently, the words *extra virgin* and *pure* do not always mean what they used to. To help you choose the proper oils, this book includes an outline of the processes by which olive oil is obtained, the factors that lessen or heighten the quality of an oil, and the current labeling practices and legislation pertaining to them. Such standards are in a state of flux, however, and a certain amount of industry self-regulation is beginning to take place, so guidelines for buying oil will continue to change from one year to the next.

As difficult as it is to unravel the new mysteries surrounding olive oil, it is a simple and more intuitive undertaking to become familiar with and appreciative of the tree from which olive oil is derived. Aldous Huxley described olive trees as "numinous." Their great height and breadth, the rock-breaking strength of their tremendous, hidden roots, the trunks through which life flows skyward to the animated leaves do suggest divinity. And, to my mind, the olive is the best of them, the most benignly numinous of trees.

Born with civilization itself, the cultivated olive tree provides the universal symbol of peace, the olive branch, and can pacify even the most restless of us if we sit in a warm, timeless olive grove. It offers gifts of great variety: light (how many wicks in bowls of olive oil have been lighted throughout history?); heat (there are few better-burning woods than olive wood, which generates 37.3 million BTUs per cord as compared with 28.2 BTUs per cord for white oak); year-round shelter from the sun and rain (the olive tree is an evergreen); and food (green, brown, purple, and black cured fruits and the sumptuous green-gold liquid). It is tenacious and undemanding, thriving in the most inhospitable terrains. And it seems to live forever. No wonder the Hebrews, the Moslems, the ancient Greeks, and the Christians made so much of this tree, its fruit and its oil.

A fascinating study could be based on tracing the interconnections of Mediterranean peoples through their culinary uses of the olive and olive oil. For example, were country bread, olive oil, and garlic combined in one geographic location and then taken systematically all over the Mediterranean, or does that combination of ingredients go together so naturally that it sprang up independently in various places? And what could be postulated about the famous north-south split that separates Spain, the Maghreb, France, Portugal, and most of Italy (those countries where the olive fruit is used extensively in traditional dishes) from Greece, Syria, Turkey, Egypt, and the Balkans (where olives are eaten in great quantity but only as small meals in themselves or as hors d'oeuvres and garnishes, but never cooked in dishes)?

That the olive is a precious part of the life of the Mediterranean is reflected by its abundant use in place names throughout the Mediterranean and around the world. From the Semitic word for olive, *zeit*, we have Zejtun in Malta; Wadi Zeit in Jordan; the Zeit mountains, a range in Egypt; Zeytindag, a mountain in Turkey; Zeytinburnu, "olive point," also in Turkey; El Zeitun, a village in Egypt; and so on. Derived from the Greek *elea* are the olive-infused place names in Europe and the Western Hemisphere. Ela is a cape and river in Cyprus; Elaia, Elaikhorion, Elaiofiton, Elaion, and Elaiotopos are in Greece; towns named Olivet can be found in France, Michigan, New Jersey, and South Dakota; Olivone is in Switzerland; towns named Oliva can be found in Argentina, Spain, and the Canaries; Oliveira dos Brejinhos is in Brazil; Olival and Olivais are in Portugal; Oliva is a mountain in Chile; the Mount of Olives is in Jerusalem; the Olivares River, a peak called Olivares de Jucar, and towns called Olivares can be found in Spain; Cerro de Olivares is a peak in Chile; Olivia is the name of towns in Minnesota and Texas.

It is probably an accurate assumption that the olive gained such importance because of its indispensable oil. It is difficult to imagine that the Mount of Olives was named after a tree because its fruit made a pleasing pickle. But in spite of the cured olive's being overshadowed by its sister product, it nevertheless is an important and irresistible creation. A bowl of *olives cassées*, placed before guests while their hostess concentrates on a *canard roti* in her Languedoc kitchen; the purple, pointed Kalamata flattering a morsel of feta cheese at a picnic in Greece; shiny, black Moroccan olives, swimming in a juicy *tagine* in Fez—all seem as indigenous to those settings as lichen on a rock. You would be hard-pressed to find a recipe for small game in Sicily that did not include olives, a platter of thrushes not replete with olives in Provence, or a breakfast table in Egypt or Syria without olives, cheese, and bread.

More and more, the various olives of France, Italy, and Greece are finding their way into delicatessens and specialty shops, as well as large markets, here in the United States. We now have the special pleasure of tasting olives shipped in their mother brine—some unpasteurized—made according to an old-country recipe, and packed in bulk straight from the barrel in their place of origin. Many Americans are tasting them for the first time and learning to prefer them to the milder black-ripe olives of California. Certain olives—the dry-cured blacks, for example—are still too bitter for the long-dormant taste buds of many of us. But the day will come when we will take the more pungent olives for granted, as we buy cracked green water-cured olives, for example, to pique the appetites of our dinner guests.

One would think that olive oil and olives would have made the trip to America long ago, with the first Mediterraneans who settled here. But circumstances dictated otherwise. Olive oil was expensive to import and many unscrupulous dealers sold bad-tasting, adulterated, or even dangerous substances as "pure olive oil." The use of olive oil did not catch on, and although it remained a staple of the Mediterranean immigrants to America, its use did not survive with succeeding generations.

Because the American olive grows well only in California (and a few other western states), and because California was late in becoming an agricultural exporter, there was no domestic supply of olive products until the early twentieth century. When California did produce oils it was for a small market, and many of the California oil makers went out of business after World War II when they were undersold by importers.

One would think, too, that with the diversity of immigrants to America, the full-bodied flavors of the Mediterranean would overcome the bland flavors of American cookery rather than the other way around. But such was not the case. When Emerson was looking for something distasteful to compare with life at sea, he chose the olive. Apparently he could get used to neither. Nor was he alone. By the time California started selling cured olives commercially, the American palate was too sleepy for anything but mild black-ripe olives, the type still widely eaten today. But our tastes have begun to change, and a growing number of small California olive producers are selling a wider variety of olives.

Americans also grew used to bland, predictable, inexpensive cottonseed oil. When we finally switched to other oils it was for health's sake, and corn and similar mild oils were chosen. In our fitness-conscious age, it has now been determined that olive oil is a neutral oil in the cholesterol controversy: It neither promotes nor decreases cholesterol buildup. Perhaps this factor, combined with America's continuing interest in so-called gourmet cooking, has encouraged a considerable number of Americans to opt for olive oil, both foreign and domestic. So far, novices tend to equate any pungency with quality, or, alternatively, blandness with subtlety. But when we shop and compare, cook and taste, our extra-virgin palates will become, I dare say, quite refined.

THE OLIVE IN
HISTORY

The whole Mediterranean, the sculpture, the palms, the
gold beads, the bearded heroes, the wine, the ideas, the ships, the
moonlight, the winged gorgons, the bronze men, the philosophers—
all of it seems to rise in the sour, pungent taste of these black
olives between the teeth. A taste older than meat,
older than wine. A taste as old as cold water.

−Lawrence Durrell, *Prospero's Cell*

THE OLIVE TREE, OLEA EUROPAEA, HAS A HISTORY ALMOST
as long as the history of Western civilization. In fact, archeologists
at a site in Spain found an olive seed that carbon-dating showed
to be eight thousand years old. Its development was one of civilized man's first accomplishments. How odd that no philosopher or historian
has had the good sense to solve the considerable problem of defining civilization by saying that the first civilized man was the one who developed the
olive, that civilization is an advanced state of human society made possible
by the olive. Since its development, the olive has been a symbol of peace and
of life's bounty, the subject of mythology, a source of light, and the very flavor of the Mediterranean.

The wild olive, or oleaster, grows in most of the countries of the Mediterranean and, in its numerous varieties, in southern and eastern Africa,
southwest Asia, and other areas. It is an unimpressive, straggly plant, which
bears tiny, inedible fruit, and has little resemblance to the magnificent *O.
europaea.*

The century in which husbandmen first cultivated *O. europaea,* and
whether it was developed from the oleaster, remain mysteries. It may have been
first cultivated independently in two places, Crete and Syria. The earlier development is generally conjectured to have been in Syria, probably by a Semitic
tribe, perhaps as long as five thousand years ago. The Egyptians called the olive
by a Semitic name, suggesting they were introduced to it by the people of the
Levant (the area bordering on the eastern Mediterranean).

By biblical times, the olive was already growing in great abundance
in the land of Canaan (an area that roughly approximated what was later

Palestine), for there are innumerable biblical references to its harvest and instructions for its cultivation. In Canaan, olives and olive oil were used from remotest antiquity for food, cooking, oil, medicine, salve, lamp fuel, and, most important, anointment. Exodus 30:22–33 reads: "Moreover the Lord spake unto Moses, saying, Take thou also unto thee principal spices . . . and . . . olive oil . . . And thou shalt make it an oil of holy ointment, an ointment compound after the art of the apothecary: it shall be a holy anointing oil. And thou shalt anoint the tabernacle of the congregation therewith, and the ark of the testimony." Note that the text specifies olive oil for the making of the unction that makes one holy. The Roman Catholic, Orthodox, and other churches still use perfumed oil made with olive oil for important rituals. *Chrism*, from which the word *Christ* is derived, means "anointed" and therefore "holy."

The olive was a symbol of safety and a harbinger of plenty for Noah when the ". . . dove came in to him in the evening; and, lo, in her mouth was an olive leaf pluckt off." Jerusalem was founded at the foot of the Mount of Olives; Gethsemane, the garden outside of Jerusalem, means "oil press" (*gathsemen*). God blessed mankind, says the Old Testament in Psalms 104:15, with "wine that maketh glad the heart of man, and oil to make his face to shine."

By the third millenium B.C., Egypt was importing two olive oils, one from Syria, the other from the west side of the Nile Delta. She did grow her own olives, but they were known only for their flesh, the oil apparently being of an inferior sort. Egyptian depictions of olive trees date from 2000 B.C., and three-thousand-year-old mummies are preserved with oil, among other things, and adorned with olive branches. Cured olives were left in the tombs of the Pharaohs for food in the afterlife. In Roman times, the Egyptian olive groves of the oasis of Fayyum were quite famous. But the cultivation of olives never became as widespread in Egypt as it did in the North African countries to the west.

Early representations of olive twigs in Minoan art suggest that olives were being grown on Crete as long ago as 2500 B.C. Because there is no indication of contact between the Levant and Crete at that time, one might conjecture that the two areas developed olive cultivation independently. The derivations from the two names for olive would support that theory: The Semitic name *zayt* became *zayith* (Hebrew), *zaita* (Aramaic), *zait* (Arabic), and *dzita* (Armenian), and spread south and west through the Levant and the Maghreb (northwestern Africa); the Cretan word *elaiwa* became *elaia* in classical Greek. It appeared in Latin as *oliva*, and then in Celtic languages (as *olew*, for example, in Welsh), and spread north and west throughout Europe.

A remarkable feature at the palace of Knossos was the Room of the Olive Press, with open pipes that fed into storage vats. The amphorae in which the oil was stored exist to this day. Olive oil became an important trade commodity for the Minoans, who probably shipped olive cuttings to Greece, the north coast of Africa, and other locations in the very ships that carried the oil. Samos, on the Minoan sea route to the Gulf of Smyrna, means "planted with olives."

Greek mythology describes how the precious olive tree was brought to Greece: Zeus had promised to give Attica to the god or goddess who made the most useful invention. Between the horse that Poseidon produced–beautiful, rapid, and capable of pulling heavy carriages and winning wars–and the olive tree that Athena produced–with oils that could illuminate the night, soothe wounds, and offer nourishment–Zeus chose the more peaceful invention and Athena became the goddess of Athens. A son of Poseidon tried to wrest the olive tree Athena had planted from the rock in which its roots were embedded, but wounded himself in committing the impious act and died. That rock is the Acropolis, where the original olive tree was guarded by soldiers. Aristides

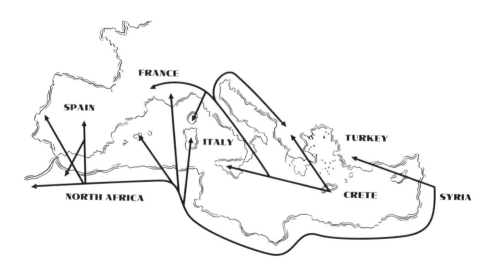

The spread of olive cultivation after the development of the domesticated olive in Crete.

said the center of Greece is Attica; the center of Attica, Athens; the center of Athens, the Acropolis. Taking things a step further, the center of the Acropolis must be the sacred olive tree.

When olive oil was first imported into Greece, in the pre-Homeric era, it was used as a costly anointment and as a component of perfumes. Its use in lamps became widespread somewhat later, and it was later still that olive oil became essential to Greek cookery. The olive "berry," however—pickled, brined, and highly seasoned—is referred to many times by Homer in *The Odyssey*, as is the olive tree. It is assumed, therefore, that cuttings were first introduced into Greece around the tenth century B.C., at which time it was realized that the calcareous soil of Greece, which had proved inhospitable to many other crops, was well suited to the undemanding olive tree.

By the seventh century B.C., olive orchards were well established on the limestone hills of Attica. By the beginning of the sixth century B.C., the great statesman Solon had enacted laws protecting the olive trees of Athens. Inspectors checked monthly to see that no trees had been cut down; anyone convicted of doing so was executed. Herodotus, in the fifth century B.C., described Athens as a vast center of Greek olive culture. Oil was produced in such abundance that it became one of the major exports. Its sale was profitable indeed. Greece also marketed molded terra-cotta oil lamps abroad and spread techniques for olive cultivation and olive curing over the whole of the Mediterranean. (The area around Aix-en-Provence, for example, was one place where Greek cuttings took root.)

The olive branch became a symbol for the Greeks. Olive-leaf wreaths adorned the brows of accomplished soldiers as well as scholars; tombs unearthed in the 1930s revealed wreaths of gold olive leaves. A frieze on the Parthenon depicts Athena's olive tree and victorious athletes receiving olive branches and bowls of olive oil. Ancient navigators protected themselves from the wrath of Poseidon by placing an olive branch between the hands of an image of their tutelary god. Athena's olive, having defeated Poseidon once, could only strengthen their god's protective power. The olive tree was so revered in Greece that it is said only virgins and chaste men were allowed to cultivate it. An oath of chastity was demanded of those who took part in the harvesting. A special wreath of olive branches, wrapped with wool, was carried by singing boys during harvest festivals, and was later hung on house doors. Olive branches dipped in purifying water were used in funeral ceremonies.

The olive was an icon for the Romans just as it was for the Greeks. They too mingled its leaves in their triumphal crowns. And "wine within and oil

THE CURATIVE OLIVE

Other generations and civilizations thought they knew instinctively what was good for them. They followed on faith (and superstition) the recipes for medicaments that were handed down to them. Olive oil, and other products and parts of the olive tree such as leaves and branches and gum from the trunk, are among those natural ingredients for remedies that have been around for hundreds or thousands of years. The first use for olive oil was as an anointment, it is generally believed, not as food or fuel: It was a soothing lubricant and emollient, and its application was so important it became a religious rite. In an Egyptian medical text dating from 1550 B.C., olive oil is listed among seven hundred therapeutics, and was taken orally as well as being rubbed into the skin.

As long as olive oil has been used as a medicine in and of itself, it has also been used to convey other curatives. And its use is as current as any recent *U.S. Pharmacopoeia*. Olive oil is useful for its ability to penetrate into the follicles, to shield against infection, and to protect wounded or irritated internal or external tissues. It is even injected intramuscularly, to convey medicines, because it is so easily assimilated.

without" became the happy formula for Roman well-being. Having learned from the Greeks the use of oil in gymnasiums, the Romans took it to extremes. Pliny complained that scrapings of oil and sweat from the great athletes were being sold by the gymnasiums for sixty thousand sesterces for use in medical plasters and emollients.

With their ascendancy, the Romans continued developing all aspects of olive cultivation and curing, and olive oil production. After inventing the screw press, they began producing olive oil as it was to be produced for the next two thousand years. Two hemispherical pieces of stone were attached to an axle set atop a post in the middle of a circular trough; as the stones turned, the olives were crushed. The oil was then extracted by a press (*torcular*), either a screw type or a more primitive type, including one with two logs against which wedges were hammered to exert pressure. (That latter ancient method is still in use in small villages in Tunisia.) After the oil was extracted, the water from the olives' flesh and sediment settled out in holding tanks; then the oil was stored in large, clean urns. (The twentieth-century centrifuge, which separates the water from the oil, is the only new development in the production of some of today's finest olive oils.)

As olive oil became more widely used in cooking, the standards for judging it were established. Cato explained that for Romans, the finest oil was "bitter oil"—that made from "white" olives (small, immature olives) picked in September. Oil from green, December-picked olives (*oleum viride*) was good-quality table oil. The oil pressed from black olives was used at the table by common people, and for lamps and anointment. The fruit for fine table oil was held for only a short time after harvesting lest it become rancid, then its pulp was subjected to moderate force. The first pressing produced the finest oil; the product lost quality as additional force was applied during the second and third pressings. The lowest quality oil was that obtained from fruit that had rotted, been damaged by vermin, or was so dirty it had to be washed with hot water.

The area that grew the best oil olives was thought to be Venafra in Samnium (Campania). Rome imported oil from Spain, Tunisia, and Istria, often as payment for taxes, although its own oil was considered the best. A fourth- to second-century B.C. cookbook entitled *De re coquinaria*, however, gives a recipe for faking the high-priced Liburnian oil from south of Istria: in Spanish oil, steep pounded helenium, cypress root, fresh bay leaves, and salt.

In Rome, pickled and cured olives were eaten in large quantities. They were particularly enjoyed as hors d'oeuvres and were thought by some to be an aphrodisiac. The Romans cured olives at all stages of ripeness. Often, the bitter glucosides were leached by soaking the olives in a wood ash paste. The green olive was preserved in salt brine; or it was mashed and soaked in frequently changed water baths, then soaked in a salt brine flavored with vinegar, fennel, and other seasonings. Sometimes sweet wine or honey was substituted for the vinegar. Half-ripe olives were picked with their stalks and allowed to cure in olive oil. Ripe olives were sprinkled with salt and held for five days, after which time the salt was shaken off and the olives dried in the sun. Sometimes pitted ripe olives were cured in jars filled with oil and coriander, cumin, fennel, rue, and mint. Such olives were referred to as oil salad and were eaten with cheese. Olives have been found still preserved in the ruins of Pompeii.

There were also olive cakes called *sampsa*, made from pressed olive pulp flavored with salt, cumin, anise, fennel, and olive oil. The rustic dish was hawked on the streets by strolling vendors and, supposedly, would last two months before going rancid.

A look through the recipes in *De re coquinaria* uncovers a sauce for boiled chicken made of pepper, cumin, thyme, fennel, mint, rue, asafetida, vinegar, dates, honey, *liquamen* (a fish sauce), olive oil, and salted olives. In a second chicken dish, chopped fresh olives are stuffed into the bird, which is then sewn closed and boiled. The olive stuffing is removed and discarded when the chicken is done. In a vegetable dish, cabbage is arranged in a shallow pan and dressed with liquamen, oil, wine, cumin, pepper, chopped leeks, caraway, coriander, and olives, then boiled.

By the time Rome fell, the olive tree was flourishing in all the temperate climates within the Roman Empire. Olive orchards were so common in Spain that Hadrian adopted the olive branch to symbolize Roman Hispania. The Moors found the tree thriving in Catalonia. Olive culture was at its height in Tunisia during the Roman occupation. (Rome taxed the province three hundred thousand gallons of olive oil yearly, and by the time the Arabs conquered the territory, olive orchards covered over two million acres.)

A curious pattern began to develop in the cuisines of the Mediterranean. In Greece and in the countries of the Levant, the fruit of the olive came to be used only as an appetizer, albeit in great abundance. But in the Maghreb and the northwestern parts of the Mediterranean, olives were added freely to dishes; in Morocco, in fact, many pungent stews, called *tagines*, are described as "smothered in olives." Oddly, the oil itself is rarely seen in Moroccan cuisine, yet it is used quite a lot in the countries of the Levant, as it is, of course, in Italy, Greece, Spain, and Portugal.

In spite of the importance of olives and olive oil around the Mediterranean, olive cuttings were not again taken a great distance until 1560, this time to Peru by the Spaniards. In the 1700s, Franciscan fathers brought the olive to Mexico, and then north into California; but it was not until the late 1800s that California commercially developed olive cultivation. Thomas Jefferson was one of many horticulturists who tried to grow the worthy tree at home, but the climate at Monticello—like the climate of England, where similar attempts had been made—was inhospitable. The olive was introduced successfully in Australia over a hundred years ago, and was taken to South Africa in 1903 by an Italian named Costa. But most of the world's olives are still grown near the Mediterranean, where the acquired taste for olives has been with its growers for hundreds of generations, and might by now—one never knows—have found its way into the gene pool.

Records of the commercial role of olive oil through the Middle Ages until modern times show that once the olive tree was established, its products became essential throughout the Mediterranean and the world. Olive oil illuminated Mediterranean homes well into the nineteenth century (and in some places into the twentieth), when it was replaced by coal and petroleum oils. Olive oil was used for making soap all around the Mediterranean and is still a common fat used in soap making. It was a prime lubricant for the machines that powered the Industrial Revolution—two thousand years after it was first used as axle grease by the Romans. And jewelers to this day polish their diamonds with fine olive oil.

EARLY OLIVE DISHES

Two recipes collected by Charles Perry, a foremost scholar on the cuisines of the world and their history, give an idea of how olives were used in the thirteenth century:

From a Syrian recipe: Take olives from Palmyra (black for preference), remove the pits, and "sift," mixing with cardamom and ground walnuts. Sprinkle with coriander, toasted walnuts, and salted lemon, knead together, and put in a jar.

From a Iraqi recipe: Take ripe or green olives (black are better) and crush and salt them. Turn them over every day until their bitterness disappears, then put them on a tray of woven sticks for a day and a night until dry. Pound garlic and dry thyme with an equal weight of walnuts. Put the mixture on a low fire, and put the tray of olives on the same stone in an oven, close the door, and leave a whole day. Stir several times so that the aromatics circulate in them. Take out and season with sesame oil, crushed walnuts, toasted sesame seeds, garlic, and thyme.

THE OLIVE IN AMERICA

pim o'la (pim o′ la) *n.*

An olive stuffed with pimiento.

—*Webster's New International Dictionary of the English Language*

What's in a name?

—Shakespeare

MERICANS HAVE HELD UP WELL UNDER THE STRAIN OF isolation. Being out here in the middle of the Atlantic (or Pacific, depending upon your point of orientation) away from our cultural roots, we have developed our own music, our own architecture, our own sports, and, of course, our own olive, the pitted black-ripe.

In keeping with much of America's eating tradition, the American olive is a subtle-tasting fruit—production line all the way. When an American opens a can of super colossals, each one will be the spitting image of the fellow on the label. No deviations, no blemishes. Perfect. Americans like their "ripe" olives crisp, shiny, and black, in a mild, clear brine. And the bigger, the better.

Although it is the Chevy Bel Air of olives, even the black-ripe is too exotic for some Americans. The California olive industry, which produces over 99 percent of the nation's olives, is having a rough time selling olives in many of the country's major markets, especially to southerners. Nevertheless, consumption of the black-ripe olive is picking up countrywide at a consistent, if modest, rate.

If the future of the olive in America could be described as bright, its past might be described as curious. The mission fathers introduced it, land developers hawked it, the University of California perfected it, and fate conspired against its success. It was a pioneer crop in a pioneer state.

It is unlikely that the olive was brought to the missions at their founding in 1769, although the secular head in charge of establishing the settlements, José de Galvez, was far-seeing and had arranged for the shipment of seeds and grain for planting. The manifest of the ship that first brought supplies makes no mention, however, of olive seedlings. Instead, it is more likely that the olives—a variety appropriately dubbed Missio—were brought some time later, probably around 1785, for the purpose of oil production. Artisans arrived at the missions around 1795, and it was probably then that the first mills and screw presses were built.

The earliest record of oil production was by Father Lasuen in 1803, who wrote that some missions had begun harvesting olives and that Mission San Diego had produced some very good oil. In 1834, the missions were secularized and their orchards largely neglected, although there are records that at some ranches, the Peralta Ranch, for example, Indians still tended the trees. Decades later, cuttings were made from the trees at the San Diego and San Jose missions by enterprising California nurserymen.

For a number of reasons, not the least being that "not one American in ten thousand had tasted olive oil" (*Sacramento Bee*, 1896), and therefore little market existed for it, olives were slow to gain acceptance after the missionaries left. An 1855 agricultural report listed only 503 commercial olive trees in the state. An oil mill at Camulos in Ventura County, built in 1871, was probably the first to be constructed outside the missions. Slowly, however, a market for olives started growing with the newly arrived non-Spanish immigrants. In fact, the olive became one of those exotic crops offered out-of-staters as an excellent investment, made all the more enticing because it could not be grown in the East, Midwest, or South.

By 1876, the number of trees had increased to 5,603. By then, many energetic young pioneer growers had decided to try olives, and there were many reports of successful plantings to encourage them. Frank and Warren Kimball were the first to plant on a large scale. In 1885, they planted a large farm in National City with cuttings taken from the old trees at nearby Mission San Diego. The Quito Ranch near Los Gatos in Santa Clara County had its own mill and, at eighty acres, the largest planting in central California. There, a few of the olives were pickled, but most were crushed for oil. (At Quito, black scale, even now one of the state's major olive pests, was treated with whale-oil soap.) By 1885, hopeful speculators had planted olive orchards in Livermore (with transplants from Mission San Jose), Riverside, South Pasadena, Los Angeles, Berkeley, Sacramento, Auburn, Napa, and Solano.

The 1896 United States Department of Agriculture Yearbook stated that in 1894 over four hundred thousand olive trees had been ordered from nurseries in Pomona alone. It is probable that a good portion of those trees were never planted; still, the orders show that many people considered the olive a potential gold mine. By the late 1800s, the olive had become a farming fad. Unfortunately, the oil produced by the new olive farmers could not compete with the much cheaper European imports, and the outlook was not bright for a better market opening at the beginning of the twentieth century.

In the early 1890s, Warren Woodson bought fifty thousand acres of railroad land-grant property near Corning, in the hot northern Sacramento Valley. He planted apricots, peaches, plums, cherries, and Mission olives. Then, advertising in church circulars and at the World's Colombian Exposition, held in Chicago in 1893, he attracted midwesterners and easterners who wanted to become farmers in California, the land of opportunity. Indeed, the town of Corning still has an unusually high number of churches per capita, thanks to the ministers and deacons of various denominations attracted by Woodson's church advertisements.

During the first few years, many of the Corning plantings were wiped out by high temperatures and drought. The hearty olive trees, however, survived. So Woodson quickly bought all the olive trees he could find, including a batch of imported trees from Spain, and replaced the more delicate crops with olives. (He planted the imported trees reluctantly, later to discover they produced a larger, albeit less oily, fruit than the Missions. They were Sevillanos, the variety that produces today's super colossals.) The new residents of Corning, the first olive-growing community in the state, found themselves farmers of one crop, the olive.

Meanwhile, in the Central Valley, near a town called Lindsay in Tulare County, the olive was catching on, but in a more offhand way. There, the new crop was citrus. Olive trees served merely as ornamentals or windbreaks for the citrus trees. The early olive trees in Tulare were Missions, and they thrived among the well-irrigated citrus. In some hill plantings the citrus did so poorly they were replaced with olives, which would endure in poor, calcareous soils. It was soon well known that olives thrived around Lindsay, but because there was no sure market for olive oil or brine-cured olives during the nineties, the farmers of Lindsay continued to plant citrus and other fruit crops. When a method for canning was perfected more than a decade after the turn of the century, and a popular new black-ripe olive had been developed to assure a market for the California cured olive, Lindsay and the surrounding area became the most heavily planted olive region in the state.

The nineties also saw the arrival of an Illinois woman named Freda Ehmann. In 1892, she came to California on the advice of her son, who owned an olive orchard about fifty miles from the Corning Colony in Oroville. When the Ehmanns' trees first bore fruit in 1897, Mrs. Ehmann contacted Professor Eugene Hilgard, an agriculturist at the University of California at Berkeley, requesting a recipe for processing ripe olives. Using Professor Hilgard's method for lye-curing, she pickled olives on the back porch of her daughter's home in Oakland. It was that mild-flavored "ripe" olive that was to become the olive of California, and of America.

Mrs. Ehmann's aggressive selling of the product, in barrels and glass jars, first to grocers in Oakland and then across the country to the East Coast and even up to the Klondike, enabled her to form a company in Oroville in 1898. Her two-ounce jars were served at dinners aboard the luxurious Southern Pacific and Santa Fe railroads, and fancy hotels served dishes featuring the much sought-after delicacy.

Almost a decade after Professor Hilgard divulged his recipe to Mrs. Ehmann, his colleague, Professor Frederic Bioletti, perfected a process for canning olives in tin. At that time, the olive industry had grown to over two million trees in the state, and farmers desperately needed a safe canning method to enable them to better control supply. Before the tin canning method had come into wide use, however, disaster hit. In 1919 and 1920, thirty-five people in the East and Midwest died of botulism after eating black olives packed in inadequately sterilized glass jars. The lye-curing produced an alkaline brine that was a perfect medium for *botulinus* bacteria; it was almost inevitable that sooner or later a mistake would be made. After the tragic setback, the new high-temperature, high-pressure method of retorting slowly gained the trust of consumers, and the olive industry began rolling again.

California land development occurred in waves. The wave that followed Woodson's subdivision in Corning swept the state after 1910, when land was still cheap enough for developers to sell inexpensively to city dwellers who wanted to get rich quick or provide for their old age. During that time, an olive boom was rekindled in Oroville and attracted an unlikely group. Eight members of the faculty at the University of Nevada, and nine from the University of California at Berkeley—all graduates of Berkeley and from an assortment of disciplines—decided to invest together in agricultural land. For a minimal investment and the sweat of their own brows, they hoped to gain financial security for their families.

Dr. Herbert Hill, an English professor, scouted the state for an appropriate crop. He considered oranges, figs, nuts, grapes, and peaches. He decided on olives; they live forever. (Perhaps their classical history had some appeal for the professor as well.) The two engineers in the group, Dr. Charles Hyde and Dr. Bernard Etcheverry, devised a hexagonal planting design that would facilitate cultivation. In 1914, Dr. Hill; Dr. Ralph Minor, a physicist; and Drs. Young and Frandsen began blasting holes in rock and setting out little trees.

In ten years, the trees were self-supporting. Some of the professors came to Oroville in the summertime to work, and camped out in the orchards with their families. Professor Vaughn built a knotty-pine cottage, to which he retired years later. During only two years did the venture show a loss, and that was during the Great Depression.

At the same time the Berkeley group was planting in Oroville, the olive industry was establishing itself in Lindsay. After Professor Bioletti's canning procedure became famous, a small group of Lindsay growers decided to start their own cooperative processing plant. It opened in 1916, with a capacity of 125 tons per year. In 1919 it was joined by a second plant, and Lindsay was well on its way to being the olive capital of the country, to become Lindsay, "a nice town, a great olive," as the highway billboard says.

All that was left to perfect—to eliminate that troubling moment when the olive eater must get the pit from mouth to pocket—was a good pitting machine. The California olive is one of the few olives marketed without the pit; and it was Herbert Kagley, a young mechanic, who devised the first mechanical olive pitter. In 1933, at the suggestion of the plant manager of Lindsay Ripe Olive Company, Kagley designed and built the prototype for the pitter. The machine was perfected by two engineers, Drake and Alberti, and it was later pitted, so to speak, against the Ashlock pitter. But H. Kagley made the one and only original, the machine that thrust the olive into twentieth-century high society and made the martini possible.

the noblest olive of them all

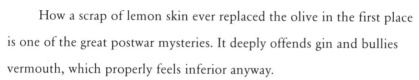

The olive's noblest function is, of course,
to keep a lemon twist out of your martini.

How a scrap of lemon skin ever replaced the olive in the first place is one of the great postwar mysteries. It deeply offends gin and bullies vermouth, which properly feels inferior anyway.

A respectable martini olive is firm, green and pitless. It is neither so large as to displace a significant quantity of liquid, nor so small as to be mistaken for a health code violation. Never does it contain a pimiento; a drink must not stare back.

What you do not do, however, is actually eat the olive. The martini consumed, the olive remains as a presence, a reminder, even a souvenir, although it is considered bad form to put it in your pocket as you might a swizzle stick or matchbook.

Each martini merits a fresh olive. The used ones can be thrown to the urchins pressing their noses against the window.

One or two uneaten olives are correct before a meal. Three frequently lead to equally uneaten meals. Four? You might as well start with a lemon twist and be done with it.

—L. R. Shannon

THE OLIVE CROP

The olive is one of the few crops in America to be grown principally on farms of moderate size. Even the few olive acreages owned by large corporations are small when compared with some of the super colossal landholdings typical of crops that are highly mechanized. Because olives are hand-harvested, and require pruning and tilling, there are few cost benefits to be realized by large-scale farming. Many of the olive orchards, particularly in northern California, are between fifteen and twenty acres.

The ideal climate for the olive is one with a long, hot summer; winter chilling sufficient to set fruit (minimum temperatures of no less than 12°F); and no late spring frosts to kill the blossoms. Olives are concentrated in eight major olive-growing counties in two areas of California. Tulare and Kern counties in the Central Valley grow almost half the olives in the state; Tehama and Butte counties in the Sacramento Valley in the north grow about a fifth. (There is a small pocket of olive acreage outside Phoenix which produces about 1 percent of what California produces.)

Five commercially important varieties of olive are grown in California: Manzanillo (pronounced man-zan-ill-o by those who grow them), Sevillano (sev-ill-ahn-o), Mission, Ascolano, and Barouni, listed in descending order of crop size. The Manzanillo is the most abundantly grown because of its fairly large size, its ease of processing and resistance to bruising, and because it ripens early, enabling growers to harvest before the early frosts. The Sevillano, sometimes called the queen olive, is next in importance because it is the largest olive and therefore fetches the highest prices at the grocery store. It was the Sevillano that confused the size designations on labels. The Mission was the first olive on the scene, with sizes designated as small, medium, large, and extra large. Thus the Sevillano, the smallest of which is larger than the largest Mission, has designations giant, jumbo, colossal, super colossal, and special super colossal. Because the Sevillano has a low oil content, it cannot be used for oil extraction as can Missions, Manzanillos, and even Ascolanos. The largest production of the Sevillano is in Tehama County, north of Sacramento.

Growing in nearby Butte County are most of the state's remaining Mission olives, the first olive to be cultivated in America. It is the smallest of the California olives, and was originally planted for its high oil yield; but because California olive oil producers found it hard to compete with importers, some of the Mission olive trees have been top-grafted to larger table olive varieties

(Manzanillos and Sevillanos). The Mission remains the olive of choice for the state's makers of cold-pressed oil, however, and many California producers are taking care to market a first-rate product.

The Italian Ascolano produces a large olive that is oilier than the Sevillano, but it bruises easily, so little acreage is planted. Still fewer acres are devoted to the Tunisian Barouni, which is a small olive shipped fresh to the East Coast for marketing to makers of home-cured olives.

PROCESSING OLIVES

Not all American-grown olives become black-ripes, nor do all American ripe-olive eaters restrict themselves to the understated canned version. A small percentage of the California olive crop fits into the "other" category—olives crushed for olive oil, sold fresh, canned as green-ripe (not blackened with oxygen), or processed in brine for sale to specialty shops and delicatessens. The exact proportion varies greatly from year to year with the amount and size of olives harvested.

Anywhere from one-twentieth to one-sixth of the total California olive harvest is processed green, depending on the size of the harvest. The salty, acidic greens are known as Spanish style, and for good reason. Most of the green olives eaten in America are imported from the world's largest olive pro-ducer, Spain, and taste just about the same as the domestic version.

The only stuffed olive manufactured in any quantity in California is the pimiento-stuffed olive. (Processes for other stuffings—onions and nuts, for example—have yet to be mechanized. Hand-stuffed olives are all from Spain, where labor expenses are lower.) The people who market olives have come up with a process comparable to that for making the maraschino cherry (a fruit whose color and flavor are extracted and to which a new color and flavor are added). What starts out as a pimiento is ground up (seeds and all) and retexturized with carrageenan, then exuded from a machine in an endless, bright red ribbon with exactly the same circumference as a Spanish-style olive's pithole. The same process is used by Spanish processors near Seville.

A few small outfits in California are marketing olives that have been cured in a mild lye solution and then bottled in a number of herb- and spice-flavored brines. Such olives are finding a market in specialty stores at high prices. Similar effects can be achieved with less expensive, canned tree-ripened olives to which garlic, red peppers, or spices are added at home. (Tree-ripened olives are picked after they have begun to turn red; they are not oxygenated, and are therefore not black as are the black-ripe olives.)

Fine California-made European-style olives are turning up in deli cases throughout the United States. One producer of such olives is West Coast Products in Orland, a town near Corning in the Sacramento Valley. Using local olives, which the company buys from the harvesters, West Coast makes a meaty oil-cured olive from dead-ripe Missions picked in March; a Greek-style olive from ripe olives picked between January and March; and Sicilian-style and cracked green olives from fall-harvested Sevillanos fermented in brine for up to six months. All the olives compare well with their imported counterparts, surpassing some of them because they have traveled less distance and have not suffered at the hands of shippers and warehousers.

CALIFORNIA OLIVE OIL

A few California companies also produce olive oil, and are competing for the rapidly growing virgin olive oil markets, which include people who care about good food and like the flavor of olive oil, and those who frequent health-food stores. The producers are recovering from the nosedive the industry took in the 1940s, when inexpensive imported oils ran most California olive oil makers out of business.

West Coast Products makes varying qualities of oil, depending on when the pressing is done, and sells it to middlemen who either blend it or sell it under their own labels. It is shipped in barrels to Zabar's delicatessen in New York City, where it is drawn from a spigot and sold to upscale cooks.

California's virgin oil makers label their products variously. Some print the year of the crop, some the variety of olive; some give nutritional information and boast the absence of preservatives. All use the designation they consider the most impressive or comprehensible—"virgin," "cold-pressed," and so on. Unfortunately, no legislation has yet been passed beyond that of making a distinction between refined oil and unrefined virgin oil. Domestic oil producers can use the designation "extra virgin" regardless of the quality of their product, as long as it is not refined. Many in the California olive oil industry would like to see a change. They sell a well-made product and would like that reflected by a credible label.

So far, even the best California oils are not yet on a par with the finest imports. The Mission olive, the best of the old crop California olives for oil production, produces an oil that is a bit flat tasting when compared to, say, a Tuscan oil. But when the oils are produced conscientiously, as at Sciabica and West Coast, the oils are quite pleasing. Unfortunately, many California companies do not restrict themselves to pressing only Missions. Some San Joaquin Valley oil producers use the culls from canneries whose chief olives are Manzanillos. The olives are often pressed when they have achieved their highest oil content, but are past their peak of quality. And most of the domestic oil presses crush the whole olive, pit and all, imparting a woody flavor to the oil.

An interesting and unprecedented development is occurring among members of the newly formed Northern California Olive Oil Council. Besides many members trying to revive old Spanish-olive groves, two nouvelle farmers, Ridgeley Evers and Nan McEvoy, have each imported about two thousand olive trees from Tuscany, of the same varieties that are used to make most Tuscan olive oil. Evers's farm is near Healdsburg, in Sonoma County; McEvoy's farm is near Petaluma in Marin County. Each has, to one extent or another, retained the assistance of Italian horticulturists and nurserymen. In fact, Dr. Maurizio Castelli (see The Olive Oil of Tuscany on page 46) is the expert who is consulting for McEvoy. Evers had his first pressing in 1993, although, being the first crop, it did not yield enough to be sold commercially. Both McEvoy's and Evers's ambitious projects hold the potential to produce some of California's finest oil and perhaps create an oil that will rival the best oils of Tuscany.

a day in the life

Let us follow a typical olive from a typical orchard near Corning—in the Sacramento Valley within view of Mount Shasta—as the olive makes its way from the tree to the can as a pitted black-ripe olive. It grows on a handsome forty-year-old Manzanillo tree that has been pruned low and spreading to make harvesting easier. The harvest begins in early October, when the olives have achieved a good size and are a bright chartreuse, just right to be made into black-ripe olives.

The pickers are migrant farm workers, few of whom speak any English. They stand on fifteen-foot, three-legged aluminum ladders, their hands partially taped for protection, and pick the olives in a milking fashion with both hands. Strapped to their bellies are buckets. Our hard olive drops into one of them. The pickers dump their buckets into wooden boxes that are stacked in the orchard rows, to be collected later by a pickup truck and taken to a receiving station where the olives are sized and graded under the supervision of the United States Department of Agriculture.

Once our olive and its peers have passed muster, they are trucked to one of the state's remaining handful of processor-canners. Although there are some cooperatives, such as Lindsay in the San Joaquin Valley, this one is

# of an olive

an independent, Bell Carter, in the town of Corning. Our olive is dumped
into a nine-ton-capacity fiberglass tub and soaked in a series of frothy lye
baths that bubble as air is pumped through the liquid. The lye baths leach
the bitter glucosides from the olives; the air "oxygenates" the olives, turning
them from bright green to solid black. Minute quantities of ferrous gluconate, the same substance used in iron tablets, fix the color. The olives are
then soaked in a mild salt brine (9.5 on the salometer), after which they go
to the pitter—a fantastic machine that performs a thousand "pitectomies"
a minute.

At this point, our pitted olive is ready for inspection, and passes
before a hundred eyes, namely, those of the women minding the conveyor
belt. Being an acceptable olive, into a can it goes, with new brine and fellow
Mammoth (i.e., medium-size) black-ripes. The can is sealed and shoved into
an enormous pressure cooker, which sterilizes the can and its contents at
262°F under careful supervision.

Our olive now waits to be freed from its container and to be waved
about on the fingertip of a happy five-year-old (the true, 100 percent authentic way of serving California olives) and eaten.

THE
EXCEPTIONAL
OLIVE OIL

Olive oil is found, not made.

—Professor Cupari

There's more to this than meets the eye.

—M. Klein

N O MATTER HOW MUCH ONE KNOWS ABOUT OLIVE OIL, THE most valuable aid to purchasing good oil is a knowledgeable merchant whose integrity is beyond question. That merchant will know the makers of the oils stocked and the circumstances under which the oils are made, and will store the oils properly. Once this merchant is found, it is up to the consumer to taste and compare, and to buy oils in small quantities until the most pleasing is found. Even then the buyer must not be limited to one label, for oils vary according to the kind of year it has been for olive production, and the kind of olives that are available to the oil manufacturer.

There are two basic rules for producing fine olive oils: the olives must be of the highest quality, and as little as possible must be done to them to extract their oil. Within the cellules of the red-ripe olive exist pockets of pure, delicious oil that is ready—without processing—to be savored.

The great olive oils of the world are produced on a small scale in the cooler climates of the olive-growing countries. Unfortunately, the small-scale producers of fine oils are finding it more and more difficult to compete with the large companies that sell refined oils. Production of true extra-virgin olive oil—olive oil made from the first cold-pressing of quality olives—has fallen precipitously since the 1960s. Fewer and fewer farmers produce oil the old, careful way.

Nevertheless, there is ample reason to believe there will be a new important market for such oils. United States consumption of first-rate oils has increased five times since the beginning of the 1980s. Although these figures represent only 12 percent of world trade, they do indicate a growing consciousness in this country, and Americans have a good choice of first cold-pressed oils. They are getting a chance to taste the fruity and fragrant light juice (and it is just that) that has been the cooking medium in much of the Mediterranean countryside for centuries. For the consumer, the difficult task is to differentiate between industrially produced, far inferior "extra-virgin"–labeled oils and the traditional cold-pressed, truly extra-virgin products.

How does one tell the good oils from the bland, refined oils, or from the poorly made, rancid-tasting oils? Which of the less expensive oils should one buy for everyday cooking? Certainly price is no criterion by which to judge; the refined-oil makers are cultivating the gourmet market, too, and often charge high prices for their oils, influencing inexperienced oil merchants or consumers to assume they have purchased the best money can buy. To the uneducated palate, even the refined olive oils are a pleasant change from the vegetable oils to which many are accustomed. After all, Americans are still cooking with flavorless oils such as canola (rapeseed) oil, safflower oil, and the like, and they consume vast quantities of cottonseed and palm oils (and animal fats as well) in mass-marketed foods bought in grocery stores or from many fast-food restaurants.

MAKING OLIVE OIL

What follows is a list of important factors that determine how good an oil will be once it reaches the table. Listing the factors may seem pedantic, but keep in mind that most everything that happens to an olive will be reflected in the flavor of its oil. The oil extracted from olives, like all fatty substances, retains the odors of almost everything near it. Those odors become flavors in the oil. (In fact, in the days of horse-powered oil mills, the farmers had to go to great lengths to ensure that the odor of the manure did not waft over the oil.)

VARIETY OF OLIVE. Olives vary as much according to variety as do apples or any other fruit. Some produce oil that is far superior to that of most others; some produce oil more plentifully. The large olives grown primarily as table olives in the hottest climates contain a small proportion of oil, which is often highly acidic. Their pits, being large and easily broken, are often crushed along with the flesh. The oil thus produced can have an undesirable woody flavor.

Some varieties famous for their oil are the Arbequiña of northern Spain, the Frantoio of Tuscany, and the Nyons of Provence (although some would classify the Nyons as a table olive). Even in the hotter climates, distinctions are made; the Zorzaleño in Andalusia and the Mission in California are favored for their oil over the larger table olives grown in the same areas.

HARVESTING. The best oil is a blend of oil from olives harvested at the red-ripe stage and a smaller proportion from green olives of a different variety. Some oil manufacturers add a few leaves to make an oil greener so it looks like that of pressings from the earlier harvest. Olives that are harvested late, when they are black, contain more oil than the red-ripe olives, but such oil is more acidic and generally of poorer quality. Much refined oil is made from the oilier, riper olives, then chemically deacidified. And some virgin olive oils with fairly high acidity, but which are still comestible without refinement, are made from riper olives.

Olives can be harvested by hand or they can be beaten from the trees and collected in nets. Green fruit is so firmly attached to the tree that it must be plucked by hand. In some areas, olives are allowed to become so ripe they fall to the ground, to be gathered by hand, by machine, or in nets. Olives that are allowed to strike the ground are bruised and collect dirt, which hastens rancidity. Oil made from bruised olives is qualitatively different (i.e., chemically different) from oil made from undamaged fruit; an experienced taster can discern the difference immediately. Oil producers who beat their olives from the trees and collect them in nylon nets claim their oil is not affected by such treatment, however.

Most olive oil experts agree that hand-harvesting is the only way to make a superior oil. In some areas, such as the Spanish countryside, pickers use small hand tools that strip the branches of their fruit; in other areas the pickers use only their hands, wearing gloves or with palms taped for protection.

Harvest methods vary greatly and affect the quality of the olive that is brought to the press. Unfortunately, few labels disclose how the crop was harvested.

STORING THE OLIVES. Newly harvested olives are usually allowed to sit for at least a few days before they are pressed. As they rest, some of the water in their flesh evaporates, making processing easier. During the storage period the olives must be kept cool; their internal temperature must never exceed 86°F. Conscientious farmers spread the olives thin for ventilation; others pack their olives under ice to prevent the fermentation caused by heat.

Olives that have been stored too long before pressing will have a very high acid content and a foul odor and flavor, making chemical refining a necessity. The large producers of refined oils frequently store their olives for long periods, enabling them to stretch out the oil production process to keep the plant operating more months of the year during daytime hours. They generally rely on refining to undo the damage done by lengthy storage.

GREEK OLIVE OIL PRODUCTION

Around the southern part of Greece,
at various sites, growing profusely on the
reddish orange sand and clay soils, are most
of the best-quality olive and oil-olive trees in
Greece. Planted at a high elevation for olives
(one thousand to thirteen hundred feet) and
subject to sea breezes, the Koroneiko olives,
just about the only variety there, are exposed
to temperature variations that are beneficial:
hot summer days that cool in the evening.

The trees are pruned small to enable
laborers to pick by hand from ladders in late
November. Such olives are green-red, not too
ripe to produce a fine oil.

As in Tuscany, each farmer brings his
harvest to the community press (*piestirio*),
along with food and drink to fortify himself
on the festive pressing day. In the small brick
buildings are crushing stones that rotate,
and a press with corrugated metal plates.
It is from such *piestirios* that importers
like Sotoris Kitrilakis of Peloponnese,
a respected company based in California,
get their excellent oil.

CRUSHING. The crushing process is the same at most mills, whether large or small. Enormous granite stones, each weighing eight tons, crush the olives into pulp. Purists maintain that a softer stone produces less bruising; and conscientious mill operators have their stones chiseled every year to correct the smoothing that occurs during crushing. Farmers take their olives to the local mill, where they are crushed and pressed.

PRESSING. In most small mills, the pulp produced by the millstones is layered on mats made of nylon or, as in the past, straw. The mats are stacked about four high, interspersed with metal disks, and then, under six hundred to eighteen hundred pounds per square inch of pressure, are pressed in a screw or hydraulic press. The better mills do this without the addition of heat or water. The oil that is thus expressed is called the first cold-pressing. If the olives are not too ripe and have been handled well, the oil will easily qualify as extra-virgin, a classification (see page 42) used in most parts of Spain and in France and Italy to denote less than 1 percent acidity. (In Catalonia, where labeling is even more strict, extra-virgin olive oil is classified as under 0.5 percent acidity.) Because chemicals can produce zero acidity, however, the designations mean little unless accompanied by strict definitions for "cold-pressed." All fine European first cold-pressed oils are well under 1 percent acidity.

In addition to using screw and hydraulic presses, to which heat and water are applied, some larger factories (and smaller ones, in growing numbers) use large centrifugal presses that spin the crushed olives as heat and water are applied. (The centrifugal press is not to be confused with the small centrifuges that separate the water from the oil after pressing in small rural mills.) Such a process extracts more oil from the pulp but damages it in the process. It is to such presses that the pulp, or *sansa*, from the first pressing at the smaller mills is taken for further processing. The oil that results must be refined to be made comestible, and is then mixed with 5 to 10 percent extra-virgin or virgin oil for flavor. Its label may read "*sansa* and olive oil."

REFINEMENT. The highly acidic or foul-flavored oils produced from *sansa* or from badly damaged fruit are placed in a series of closed vessels. Chemicals with properties similar to those of gasoline (hexane, trichlorethylene, or carbon sulfide) extract the oil by percolation. In a steam-heated still, the solvent is completely recovered by condensation. The oils that result are pale, very fluid, nonacidic, and absolutely without flavor. Mixed with 5 to 10 percent virgin olive oil for flavor and color, they can be sold as pure or virgin oil or, if the acidity is low enough, as extra-virgin oil. With a few exceptions—notably, the divine cold-pressed extra-virgin oils from the small producers—such refined oil constitutes most of the olive oil available to American consumers.

SEPARATING WATER FROM THE OIL. After the first (or in the case of the inferior oils, second or third) pressing, a percentage of the resulting fluid is water. That water is separated from the oil in a small centrifuge that spins at 1,500 revolutions per minute, or it is allowed to settle out in a large holding tank. Most olive oil purists allow for this, the only new machine in the age-old process of making fine oils. But there are a few who contend that the centrifuge damages the oil, and that the best oils are made when the water settles out naturally.

SETTLING. The new oil is a cloudy liquid, full of minute particles of fruit in suspension. Most producers allow the oil to settle for a number of weeks, usually in huge earthen jars in a cool cellar. (The oil can be kept there almost indefinitely, until it is convenient for the producer to decant and bottle, or filter and bottle, it.) The new oil is ready to use, but is particularly peppery and fruity the first two months. A few producers bottle a small portion of the new, turbid oil and sell it as "new oil" to an elite few who are particularly fond of the potent liquid.

FILTRATION. It is not essential for good-quality olive oil to be filtered. Some producers say that filtered oil keeps longer than unfiltered; some disagree and say filtration deprives the oil of flavor. Some feel that the clear oil is more aesthetically pleasing. Fine oils are usually filtered through cotton; alkaline earth filters are often used to reduce the acidity of poorer oils.

VARIABLES. Just as some vintners buy grapes from other growers, many of the small olive farmers buy olives from other growers to augment their own production. This is especially true in years when crops have been damaged by pests in one area and not in another, or when an area is affected by drought or an unusual cold spell. For example, during the winter of 1985, areas of Tuscany were hit by severe frosts and snow. The olive trees were so badly damaged that many died and none produced a harvestable crop. Some producers processed olives from other areas such as Umbria, and sold blends under labels reading "bottled by." Others stopped processing altogether and waited for damaged trees to renew themselves or for newly planted seedlings to grow to harvest stage.

The conscientious oil maker is as careful choosing the olives he buys as he is growing his own. Nevertheless, the different varieties, microclimates, and growing methods will produce oils with different characteristics. A producer might make a fruitier oil from the olives he has had to purchase one year than is characteristic of the oil usually made from his own olives.

Then too, different varieties of olives ripen at different times. If, as is common practice, a grower has three olive varieties in his orchards, he might harvest two-thirds of his crop red-ripe and one-third green. The proportion of ripe to green olives will have a marked effect on the oil, and will differ from year to year depending on the weather and the producer's olive sources.

Thus your preference for Brand X in January of one year may change to Brand Y in August or the following January. The best the consumer can do is know which brands are made well—and there are currently dozens of superb oils being imported into the United States—and to compare the exquisite olive juices continually.

THE NUTRITIVE OLIVE

The modern American, with all his patent contrivances...will never know...a full tide of health until he returns to the proper admixture of olive oil in his diet. Until he again recognizes the value and use of olive oil, he will continue to drag his consumptive-thinned, liver-shriveled, mummified-skinned, and constipated and pessimistic anatomy about...in a vain search for lost health.

—P. E. Remondino, M.D., in an essay presented at the Olive Growers' Convention, Sacramento, California, 1891.

TASTING OLIVE OILS

Here's how an olive oil expert tastes oils. He pours a little of each oil into wineglasses and compares color and fluidity. He cannot determine fattiness by appearance, but he can usually tell which olive varieties make up each oil by its color; he is rarely stumped. Then he smells an oil, inhaling deeply. He sips a little, inhales while holding the oil between his soft palate and tongue, swishes it between his upper teeth and lip and on his gums, and inhales again. He spits it out and makes his declaration: "Ugh, fatty" or "Could be from Umbria, extra virgin, but made by a big company," or "Almondy, very nice."

A wine taster may taste at least twelve, sometimes as many as twenty, different wines at a tasting, but the limit even for an expert oil taster is six or seven. Eugenio Pozzolini of Dean & DeLuca Imports of New York is one such expert. He says that fine oils are tasted horizontally, that is, on the palate. A bad, acidic oil will be sensed vertically, in the throat, and leaves a bad aftertaste and a fatty coating in the mouth.

Begin a tasting by taking a little oil and rubbing it in the palms of your hands, then putting some on the back of your hand. Smell it. Note the aroma, whether or not it is fresh and fruity. If you are a novice, know as much about the oil you are tasting as you possibly can. Leave the blind tastings for later. Start out with a good oil your merchant describes as mild—perhaps one mellowed by a year of proper storage—and less of a jolt than, say, a peppery Tuscan extra virgin. Dip a spoon into the oil and sip about half a teaspoon. If you prefer to taste the oils with food, use small pieces of steamed potato to dip into the oil; potatoes are more neutral than bread. Use slices of crisp apple to cleanse your palate between tastes.

Olive oil is certainly a matter of preference, as much a subjective choice as with any condiment. Nevertheless, the most frequent contenders for best oil among most olive oil cognoscenti are the cold-pressed extra-virgin oils of Provence, Liguria, Tuscany, and Peloponnisos. Connoisseurs who favor the Ligurian oil would say that it has more finesse than the oils of Tuscany, more life than the oils of Provence. Francophiles prefer the sweetness of the "lady oils," perhaps claiming they have a more highly developed and refined sense of taste than do the lovers of the Italian oils. Experts who favor the Tuscan oils would say the peppery aftertaste adds more life, and that the oils have a singular rustic flavor and more body. Those who enjoy the Greek oil appreciate the aromatic, olivey flavors of the Peloponnesian countryside.

That the number of producers of such fine oils has fallen off so drastically is lamentable. The sad truth is that many European consumers, the major market for olive oil, would rather cook with the inexpensive refined oils of the huge olive oil companies than pay the price for the necessarily labor-intensive finer oils. The elaborate labeling laws do nothing to protect the manufacturer of carefully made oils, or the consumer who wishes to discern a well-made product by reading a label. The designations of oils from Spain, Italy, and France are based on acidity, and the acidity of an inferior product can be lowered quite easily with chemicals. There is nothing to stop the manufacturer of a deacidified refined oil from calling it extra-virgin olive oil, so long as the oil is less than 1 percent acid.

Where does that leave American consumers who would like to have access to the best oils? We are, for the time being anyway, in the happy position of being a promising market for the small producers, if not their last hope. The consumption of imported extra-virgin olive oils in the United States is expected to have risen from 20,000 tons in 1980 to 150,000 tons by 1995. The American consumer is insisting on quality products. Perhaps, as with the California wine industry, American olive oil producers will be inspired to improve their product to satisfy the increasingly discriminating American palate. There are, in fact, several northern California growers who have planted orchards to Italian seedlings, having been the first, it is believed, to legally import Italian varieties for commercial use in this century (see California Olive Oil, page 26).

And what of the refined olive oils? Admittedly, they do not compare to the cold-pressed oils. But with virgin oil added to the deodorized oil, they make a much tastier everyday cooking medium than the wholly refined oils of most vegetables or seeds, and a more appropriate ingredient for certain dishes. Because the expensive cold-pressed oils suffer when heated over 140°F, it is wasteful to use them in high-temperature cooking. I have enjoyed many fine meals prepared with refined olive oil.

The olive oil experts have their own vocabulary for describing the flavors and nuances of the oil. Almondy oil, as the name suggests, is oil reminiscent of almonds. Bland oil is light, but with hardly any flavor, characteristic of refined oils. Fatty oil is high in fatty acids and is made from damaged, old, or overripe fruit, and leaves an unpleasant coating in the mouth. Such oils can also have a slight rancid flavor. Fluid oils are not as thick as first-pressed oils and are characteristically refined oils. Fruity oil has the hearty flavor of olives that is particularly apparent in oils with a high percentage of green fruit and in newly pressed oils. Peppery oils produce a sensation somewhat like that produced by peppers, but it is not felt in the nose. Such a quality is most pronounced in new and Tuscan oils. Rustic oil is hearty and flavorful; sweetness is characteristic in lighter oils, such as those from Provence.

Generally speaking, the hotter climates produce fatty, lesser olive oils. All olive oils from a particular region, such as northern Italy, are not necessarily of the highest quality, however; nor are all Sicilian oils, for example, necessarily poor. There are pockets of cooler climates mixed in with the hot. Furthermore, a conscientious oil maker using a larger, riper olive can make an enjoyable, flavorful, honest product that might be less expensive than a deceptively labeled oil from a more prestigious, cooler district, manufactured by a corporation whose family name is not at stake.

The best insurance for the consumer is to develop the expertise to taste the quality of oils and, equally important, to find a knowledgeable merchant. Some merchants are now certifying their imported oils as being first cold-pressed. You can test the labeling on your oils by putting a small quantity in a bowl and refrigerating it for a few days. If it forms small crystallike structures it is probably extra-virgin cold-pressed; if it becomes like butter, it is probably "pit oil"; if it turns into a block, it is probably an industrially produced, chemically refined extra-virgin oil. Remember, too, newly pressed olive oil tastes best and, ideally, it is used up within a year of pressing. Look for the year of pressing on the label to avoid buying old oils.

OLIVE OIL AS HEALTH FOOD

I would not want to argue against claims
that olives are an aphrodisiac—*a chacun son
gout*—nevertheless, the cured fruit of the
olive tree cannot be construed as health food.
The smattering of vitamin E in olives and the
iron that some contain (ironically, the ferrous
gluconate added to California black olives
to fix their color is the same substance used
in iron tablets and is quite nutritious) are
completely overshadowed by the great
quantities of salt added in curing.

But the fruit that must be so tortured to
be made palatable produces, by the simplest
of methods, the purest and most healthful oil
available. Within the pulp of the red-ripe
olive are small cellules containing wholesome,
quite edible oil that can be extracted simply
by pressing. Consequently, the vitamins that
many other oils lose in chemical extraction
and heat (up to 440°F) purification are
left unspoiled in cold-pressed, virgin olive
oils, which are rich in vitamins E (and alpha-
tocopherol) and K and in betacarotenes.

IDENTIFYING AND BUYING OLIVE OIL

The labeling laws of countries with regulated denominations such as "extra virgin" (*vierge extra* in France, *extra vergine* in Italy, *virgen extra* in Spain) are not strict enough to ensure that an extra-virgin oil is made from the first cold-pressing of olives. Those three countries have the strictest regulations of any countries from which the United States imports olive oil, but their nomenclature is based solely on acidity, an inadequate criterion of quality. Although the first cold-pressing of high-quality olives does produce oils of low acidity, an equally low, or lower, acidity can be honestly claimed on labels of chemically refined oils that have been totally deacidified by alkaline solutions. Also, a refined oil, with some first-pressed oil added for flavor and color, can be labeled "extra virgin" and catch the shopper off guard. Large companies are the ones that most frequently sell the bland, refined oils, but some smaller producers in the most prestigious areas of oil production can be equally guilty.

The following are the broad designations of Italy, France, and Spain, omitting the designations of stricter areas within each country (such as Catalonia). Note that oils from these countries that bear the words *extra virgin* or *superfine virgin* are either the first cold-pressing (the best-quality oils) or the rectified oils (the last two classifications) that qualify as extra virgin by having low acidity.

Extra-virgin olive oil
Less than 1 percent acidity

Superfine (sometimes "fine") virgin olive oil
1.01 percent to 1.50 percent acidity

Fine (sometimes "regular") virgin olive oil
1.51 percent to 3 percent acidity

Virgin (sometimes "pure") olive oil
3.1 percent to 4 percent acidity

Lamp oil (not comestible)
Greater than 4 percent acidity

Olive oil
Rectified and refined lamp oil with 5 to 10 percent virgin olive oil added

Sansa and olive oil
Rectified and refined *sansa* oil (made from the pulp from first and second pressings) with 5 to 10 percent virgin olive oil added.

The regulations passed by the United States Food and Drug Administration in 1982 for oils produced in America are better worded than the European laws and clearly state that "the name 'virgin olive oil' may be used only for the oil resulting from the *first pressing of the olives* [my emphasis] and which is suitable for human consumption without further processing." The regulation further states that blends of refined and virgin oils can be labeled "pure olive oil" but not "virgin." Those regulations apply only to oils produced in this country, however, and the federal government has not yet introduced definitive labeling criteria for more than those two grades of olive oil. According to the 1982 regulations, an American oil labeled "extra virgin" need not be different from an American oil labeled "virgin." Truth-in-labeling laws covering imports are well enforced in the United States. Adulterants in oils are easily detected in a laboratory by the use of saponification values, specific gravity values, and so on.

OLIVE OIL IN THE KITCHEN

STORING OIL. Store oil in glazed clay, very clean tin, stainless steel, or glass. Do not store it in copper or iron. Plastic will impart a flavor to the oil over time. Place the container in a cool, dark place. Oil that has been affected by heat or light has a copper hue characteristic of oxidized oil. Well-stored oil can keep at least two years; some say it can keep indefinitely under perfect conditions. But remember, olive oil does not improve as its ages; it is at its best the first year after it is pressed, and at its most flavorful the first two months.

Do not refrigerate olive oil. The best oil makers say that to do so is like storing wine in a refrigerator; it interrupts the active life of the oil.

COOKING WITH OIL. If you are using olive oil to cook with, it is pointless to use your best oil, as heating changes its character substantially. Find a good-quality, less-expensive oil that is to your taste for recipes that call for cooking with oil. I use a pleasant, unfiltered extra-virgin Spanish oil for cooking; others prefer California or Greek.

The flavor of olive oil begins to change at 140°F. For that reason, fine olive oils should be added to dishes after they have been cooked, whenever possible. When barbecuing meat or fish, add the oil after cooking, unless oil is part of a marinade. Add olive oil to soups at the table. Olive oil is, in part, a condiment.

Olive oil will begin to burn at 280°F, a low temperature compared with other oils, many of which can be heated to 365°F and higher. That means for frying foods such as potatoes, whose texture depends on a high temperature, it would be better to use peanut oil or another salubrious oil with a high burning point.

REUSING OIL. Olive oil that is used for frying can be strained through cheesecloth, refrigerated, and used again, provided it has not been overheated. Do not keep olive oil that has been brought to the smoking point, as overheating produces toxins. Oil used for frying fish should be reused only for frying fish, and then certainly not more than once.

OIL VESSELS. Of the oil cruets available, the best are those that do not drip. A modern, stainless-steel cruet from Italy, which is being imported into the United States, collects the oil that would otherwise drip and funnels it back into the container. The long-spouted tin containers are pretty and more traditional, but sometimes messy. Glass cruets, or your favorite glass vessels, are fine, but must be stored in the dark.

NUTRITION. Olive oil is considered a monounsaturated oil, with 73.7 percent monounsaturated fatty acid, 13.5 percent saturated fatty acid, and 8.4 percent polyunsaturated fatty acid. Of the oils available for cooking, it is the highest in monounsaturates. It has no effect on the cholesterol level of the bloodstream. (And, as with all vegetable oils, it contains no cholesterol.) The effect of diet on serum cholesterol has yet to be determined precisely; however, it has been suggested that a diet rich in monounsaturated oil, specifically olive oil, creates a "biochemical milieu" that leads to lower serum cholesterol, which is, perhaps, the reason Greek men have far less incidence of coronary disease than American men. One tablespoonful of olive oil contains 125 calories.

THE OLIVE OIL
OF TUSCANY

Why do we make oil?

Because we always have.

– The Farmers of Tuscany

For my taste, the best olive oils now available in the United States are from Tuscany. There are currently about sixty top-notch Tuscan oils being imported from small farms in the region. Such oils are characterized by their clean, strongly fruited flavor, their pepperiness, and their so-called rustic qualities. There is no doubt that besides Tuscany there are various locations around the Mediterranean that produce oils that are as good as, if perhaps different from, the Tuscan oils.

It is not only because I have become so familiar with Tuscany and its oil production that I include this chapter; it is also because, within the years that I have been so exceedingly interested in olive oil and its production, I've come to realize that to the everyday cook the fine olive oils available, from any number of regions, have one thing in common: the means by which they are produced. So growers at a tiny farm in Catalonia, say, will extract their olive oil just as their counterparts in a Tuscan *frantoio* do, and just as their ancestors did many hundreds of years before them.

Throughout the hills of Tuscany, and in particular those of Chianti—intermixed with the lovely, profuse vines that produce the Sangiovese grape—grow the small, bleak, twisted olive trees that produce the fine oils that have established themselves in shops throughout the United States. Curious anthropologists come here to pick and sift among the Etruscan ruins. It is a land still, to a certain extent, owned by noble families whose lineages can be traced a thousand years or more. Here stretch miles of chestnut and umbrella pine forests, broken by rows of vines and clusters of well-tended olive trees, and dotted with fine old castles and the lovely *case coloniche* that were once in their domain.

In Florence, the old Tuscan center of commerce, history and the present live side by side; and in the medieval towns that crown the surrounding hills the same is true. Occasionally that affiliation is amicable, with modernity complementing antiquity, in some cases rescuing it, and sometimes tearing down the old orders that needed removing. Too often, of course, the present taints the past, adding a power line, an afternoon of brown sky, or a foreign conglomerate to fill the void left by a crumbled old fiefdom.

The old hamlet called Monti is a good case in point. It sits atop a hill; its old stone structures are inhabited by two families whose forebears' forebears lived there before them. They raise their own poultry, rabbits, and vegetables, and look after the vin santo grapes that hang in one of the ancient rooms. (Vin santo, or "holy wine," is made by hanging white wine grapes to dry for four months, then crushing the sweet "raisins" and aging the resulting wine in casks for many years.) Not a hundred yards from that room, a little below the medieval dwellings, stand gleaming, new stainless-steel holding tanks—the latest in wine technology—that contain the year's harvest of Chianti Classico for one of the area's fine wine producers.

In the Chianti countryside one is always aware of the oldness of things. Life five hundred years ago was certainly no less sophisticated than it is today. Indeed, throughout the Middle Ages and the Renaissance, and after, Chianti was of great political, intellectual, artistic, and agricultural importance. Each of the region's ancient castles, abbeys, and estates can trace its history through letters, accounts, maps, and so on, in surprisingly intricate detail. At the castle of Uzzano, for example, the walls of the tasting room where olive oil and wines are sampled are hung with documents dated hundreds of years before. A letter marked "Prato, 1398" mentions the wine of Uzzano; a prize for olive oil from an American exhibition in 1876 hangs next to a photo of a seven-foot-high, prize-winning Chianina bull raised on the estate.

Not far from the estate at Uzzano stands the Badia a Coltibuono (the Abbey of the Good Harvest), owned by Piero Stucchi-Prinetti and his wife Lorenza de' Medici. Piero's family has been the proprietor since shortly after the abbey was secularized by Napoleon. The farm is managed from the beautiful twelfth-century, castlelike pile, and produces olive oil, Chianti Classico wine, vin santo, and farm products typical of the area, such as an unforgettable chestnut honey.

The Badia is an estate of about twenty-two hundred acres, of which only a small portion is planted with olives. Another small percentage of land is devoted to grapes. The rest is pine and chestnut forest. Here, the olive trees are grown at a high elevation—fifteen hundred feet (two thousand feet is the limit for olives). Most of the abbey's seven thousand trees are of the Frantoio variety, a low yielding, cold-susceptible olive that produces one of the fruitiest, most peppery, and least fatty and acidic of the oils. Growing among the

Frantoios are some heartier Leccinos and Maraiolos, and some Pendulinas, which fertilize the Frantoios. (On some of the neighboring farms, the faster-ripening Leccino olives are harvested and cured with salt, orange peel, and fennel for table olives.) None of the olive trees is large; they stand only twenty feet from one another without coming close to touching. And at this elevation even the oldest of the trees remains small.

Like many of the old estates, Coltibuono has adopted modern techniques whenever they can ensure a better product. Dr. Maurizio Castelli, an enologist and agronomist, oversees the oil and wine production at the abbey. He has introduced new methods of production in the abbey's Chianti Classico wine making, but has left the ancient techniques for making vin santo intact. Passionate about quality, he has left less to chance with the olive oil production than was done in the past.

Maurizio explains that new plantings are being made on slopes rather than the traditional terraces, thus permitting the use of tractors to till the soil. He quotes the old adage, "The olive tree is generous to the generous cultivator," and says that the soil must be turned twice a year. Although the trees can do fairly well by themselves on this arid, rocky soil, Maurizio uses nitrogen and organic fertilizers, and says that some of his neighbors have even introduced drip irrigation. The northeastern winds that seem so harsh to us are a blessing because they help stave off the olive's natural pest enemies. (That is essential because pesticides cannot be used on an oily fruit that retains chemicals and odors.)

He trains his workers particularly well in pruning. The old ways were not the best ways, and Maurizio's scientifically developed methods alleviate the previous tendency to "alternate bear," to get the most from each tree. Unlike the grape, the more the olive bears, the better the fruit.

At the abbey, as at most of the olive oil-producing farms in Tuscany, the olives are picked when they are a lovely red ripe. (Although they have a higher oil content, the riper purple and purple-black olives are much "fattier" and more acidic and are to be avoided when making fine olive oil.) The olives become red during November and December, when the days are their shortest and the air is raw. The silver leaves of the small, wind-bent trees look gray against the misty sky. The same families that only two months before had picked grapes in the autumn sun are now warmly dressed against the cold for the arduous hand-harvest. The pickers pluck the olives one by one, much as they did hundreds of years ago, lest the olives be bruised or the trees damaged.

As are most of the olive crops in the area, the abbey's harvest is processed at a local *frantoio* (after which the variety of olive is named). The operation at

Pisignano is like many of the local mills, including the one to which Coltibuono takes its oil. It is run by Valerio Balbieri; about a hundred and fifty farmers depend on him for their pressings. Balbieri's workers are paid in part in oil, as are many of the agricultural workers in Tuscany. Their tools lie atop an ingeniously constructed receptacle that catches all the oil that drips off the scoops and cups. During December and January, the small tile-lined building is alive with festive activity twenty-four hours a day, with the exception of eight hours at Christmas and eight hours on New Year's. The farmer whose olives are being crushed and pressed watches, drinks wine, and jokes with other farmers and the mill workers while the oil is extracted from his harvest. At Pisignano, the giant new eight-ton stones are run by machinery, not by oxen or "blind" horses as they were in the past. The crushed olives, or "mash," are layered on strawlike mats, and the old mechanical presses do their job. Then the water is spun from the oil by the small centrifuge, and the proud farmer soaks a piece of bread in his oil, tastes it, and pronounces his the best oil ever pressed.

College-trained Maurizio from the abbey is no less proud of his product than are the earthier-looking farmers. The abbey's oil, once tasted, is taken back to be stored in *orci*, the enormous old earthen urns traditional in Tuscany for hundreds of years and, like the *orci* of most of the oil makers of the area, they wear the patina of oils from many years' harvests. The oil sits in cool, dark caverns, not unlike wine cellars, until it is bottled with a decrepit, antique-looking bottling machine.

But before the new oil is poured into the lovely, tall, hand-blown bottles of the abbey, it is filtered through cotton. The procedure is not wholly necessary, but the turbid apearance of the unfiltered product is, for many, less attractive than the clear, green-gold filtered oil. Maurizio maintains that filtration allows longer storage.

The fine, fruity, peppery oil is a staple in the Stucchi-Prinetti household. It is served daily from a cruet at the dining room table, at special dinners and everyday lunches alike. The oil is poured, along with a little of the abbey's piquant wine vinegar, over salads of arugula and lettuces fresh from the kitchen garden, or unstintingly into minestrones. Accompanied by the abbey's Chianti, dinner is preceded by crude crackers made at the baker's in nearby Gaiole with Tuscan oil, and followed by hard, Gaiole-made *biscotti* dunked in sweet vin santo. Chianti is indeed the land of *la dolce vita*.

OLIVES AT THE TABLE

I know of nothing more appetizing on a very hot day than to sit down in the cool shade of a dining room with drawn Venetian blinds, at a little table laid with black olives, *saucisson d'Arles*, some fine tomatoes, a slice of water melon, and a pyramid of little green figs baked in the sun . . . In this light air, in this fortunate countryside, there is no need to warm oneself with heavy meats or dishes of lentils. The Midi is essentially a region of carefully prepared little dishes.

—Pampille
(pen name for Madame Léon Daudet,
in Elizabeth David's *French Provincial Cooking*)

PLUCKED FROM THE TREE, AT ANY STAGE OF RIPENESS, THE olive is acrid and inedible because of the glucoside that is abundant in its flesh. It seems less promising a food than an uncooked artichoke. Man has lived up to the challenge of the olive many hundred times over, however, by producing uncountable variations of delectable cured olives.

How it was discovered that leaching makes the olive edible no one knows. Perhaps one day some olives fell from a tree atop a cliff onto a Grecian beach, lay exposed to the sun and salty water, were spied by a particularly hungry ancient, and an important culinary discovery was made. However it first happened, there are now five basic ways to leach the glucoside from olives: oil-cured are soaked in oil from one to several months; water-cured are soaked in water, rinsed, and soaked again for many months; brine-cured are soaked in a salt-brine solution from one to six months; dry-cured are cured in salt from one to several months, sometimes rubbed with oil and called oil-cured; and lye-cured are soaked for a few days in a strong alkaline solution made most often with lye, but sometimes with wood ash or caustic soda.

After the glucoside is vanquished, the relatively simple task of adding seasoning is all that remains. Some unusual, perhaps unique, methods for curing olives can be added to that list of techniques. In the French Midi, olives called Fachouilles are cured in the sun. As would be expected, they are quite bitter; they are a rural olive and are not exported. A more famous, but still unusual, method for curing olives produces *olive schiacciate* in Calabria and

Sicily. The olives are picked green, crushed, then cured in oil, and are served as a salad. These pungent olives are also unavailable abroad. Descriptions of a variety of cured olives from olive-producing countries around the Mediterranean follow.

EASTERN AND SOUTHERN MEDITERRANEAN. These areas produce olives that are not directly marketed in the United States, but Italian merchants will sometimes market these olives as their own. In spite of the fact that Syrians, for example, cure olives at all stages of ripeness and produce a variety of good olives, their products are sold almost solely at domestic marketplaces. (Local housewives store them in lightly vinegar-flavored water and float olive oil on the surface.) The same can be said of Tunisia's Ouslati and Meski olives. Among all the African olives, only Morocco's have appeared in North American deli cases. Morocco makes hundreds of different olives, which are used extensively in Moroccan cuisine, but I have seen only two here: a round, brine-cured olive (see glossary on page 62), and a meaty, dry-cured olive, perhaps the best of its kind available.

FRANCE. It has been said that in Provence alone there are three hundred different types of olives available in village markets. The French are extraordinarily imaginative when it comes to inventing ways to process and flavor olives, although one of their most famous olive varieties, the Picholine, is named after an Italian expatriate, Picholini, who is said to have introduced ash-curing to France. *Olives en saumure* are red-ripe, needle-pricked olives, leached in water for ten days before they are soaked in brine; *olives farcies* are variously stuffed olives; *olives cassées* are cracked green olives, cured in water, then marinated in a salt brine with fennel.

One advantage the French have in producing splendid olives is a splendid climate—a colder one that produces more flavorful, albeit smaller, olives than do the hotter Mediterranean climates. The famous olives of France—Picholine, Nyons, and Niçoise—are tiny when compared to the plump Gordal of Spain, but have superior texture and flavor. Other French varieties are Rougeon, Redoutant, and Coucourelle.

GREECE. The number-two table-olive producer in the world, Greece exports a much wider variety than Spain. The United States imports more types of brine-cured olives from Greece than from any other country. The large olives of Greece are picked at all stages of ripeness. Their most famous green olive is the Agrinion, a cracked olive the color of a green sea. The Amphissa is a purple olive, indicating it is picked almost dead-ripe, and is brine-cured. On the islands around Mykonos, farmers cure their large olives themselves and produce one that is similar to the Kalamata in flavor. They slit it in three places, soak it in water for two weeks, then store it in salty brine (brine is judged salty enough when a whole raw egg floats in it) to which a little vinegar is added after eight hours.

ITALY. Both small and large olives are produced in Italy because of its wide range of climates. In the oil-olive country around Tuscany, farmers use the small Leccino to make a table olive flavored with orange peel and fennel. Tiny, black, wrinkled olives are sold in the area around Rome; on the city's streets, mild, medium-size *olive dolce* are sold in paper cones. Castellamare is famous for its black olives. From Liguria come the subtle, small, ripe olives that are aged eight months in brine. One of the Gaeta olives is tiny, purple, and brine-cured; another is larger, meatier, and dry-cured.

SPAIN. Most of the world's table olives come from Spain. The plain around Seville in Andalusia has the perfect climate and soil for the mass production of olives. The common varieties are the Manzanillo (which was transplanted with great success to America), the fat Gordal (which is much like the Sevillano, another transplant to America), and the Picual. Well over two million metric tons of olives are produced in Spain yearly by large companies (at least one of which is American-owned), and about two-thirds of the crop is converted to the green factory-processed olives we see most often, stuffed and packed in glass jars. While still green, they are beaten from the trees with sticks by peasant workers and farmers, given a short lye cure, then fermented in salt brine and preserved with lactic acid. All that remains of the olive is its shape and firm texture, the olive flavor having been replaced by salt and acid.

The Spanish have developed state-of-the-art machinery: a pitter that processes seventeen hundred olives a minute. (California olive producers brag about a one thousand-pit-per-minute machine.) The Spanish also manufacture the same reconstituted, gelatinous pimiento the Americans do for stuffing their green olives with, and are working on a similar substance made with anchovies. A machine that replaces the top of the pitted olive will cover the implantation without leaving a mark, making the new, anchovy-stuffed olive one of the great accomplishments of the industrial age. The hand labor necessary for stuffing olives with onions and nuts has yet to be replaced by machinery, however.

It is unfortunate that no rural brine-cured olives are exported from Spain into the United States. There do remain small olive farmers in Spain—and not only in Andalusia, but farther north in Catalonia—who grow Arbequiña and other more oily olives and cure them for local consumption. Many Spaniards think of the flavor of cracked green farm olives when they think of Christmas, for that is the time of year when the new olives are first ready to eat.

pitfalls

Many recipes call for pitted, brine-cured olives. Because such an article is rare indeed (the only one I know of is a Kalamata imported by Peloponnese), I set out to find a suitable implement to produce my own pitted olives in no time. I made a complete tour of the stores in my area. All I could find was something called a cherry pitter, and a French device (probably of medieval design) I found in New York labeled a *denoyauteur*.

The cherry pitter worked perfectly well on certain ripe olives that were not too soft, not too hard, had a loose pit, and were of a precise, moderate size. When I tried pitting a Picholine with it, I poked a hole in my thumb big enough to stuff a pimiento into. The cherry pitter was worse than useless.

The *denoyauteur*, on the other hand, worked well on all the smaller, ripe, brine-cured olives. If you come across one, and are in the habit of making Provençal *tapénades*, it will be worth the investment. I have read of a *chasse noyaux* that one can buy in France and is reputed to be adept not only at cracking but at pitting olives. From the general sound of the words *chasse noyaux*, my suspicion is that the instrument is likely to crush any olive it gets its teeth into.

Still, cutting the meat from the pit with a sharp paring knife is not so tedious a task. With certain cracked and slit olives, the pits can be removed easily without the aid of a knife, and the olives remain in one piece, sort of.

AN OLIVE GLOSSARY

The following index of olives represents most of the general types now available in specialty shops around the country. It is by no means exhaustive, nor does it touch on the marinades and herb flavorings prepared at individual stores. Furthermore, a greater variety of olives is being imported all the time. This index simply gives a sampling of the many curing procedures, sizes, and shapes American cooks now can count on as ammunition in their culinary arsenal.

Olives that are shipped to the United States come either in plastic, five-gallon containers or in large, beautifully decorated cans, packed in their cloudy mother brine. The trip takes about six weeks from farm (one would hope) to retail outlet. Because olives are "alive" (they continue to ferment in their brine), shippers have sustained some losses when gases cause cans to explode. Inventive packers have designed cans with valves to allow the gases to escape. Others bring the containers up to 160°F to slow the fermentation. (Higher temperatures would soften the olives or destroy some of the subtle flavors present in their brine that are caused by airborne yeasts that help them ferment.) The longer an olive is allowed to ferment in its own brine, the less bitter and more intricate its flavors will become. Some olives age eight months, others as little as two months.

Accurate names for the olives have yet to be devised. Most are sold by the name of the area or town of origin (e.g., Gaeta and Niçoise); several are named for the variety of olive from which they are made (e.g., Picholine and Salona); still others are sold according to the method of curing (e.g., Greek and Sicilian styles). Confusion arises when more than one olive comes from one place, as is possible with all olives, no matter how small the place of origin; when one variety is cured many different ways; when one person's Greek-style olive is another person's dry-cured; or when olives are deceptively labeled (many olives said to have come from Gaeta, for example, are actually from less prestigious areas of the Mediterranean). That is why it is a good idea to sample olives before buying. Store owners are usually very obliging, and tasting will save you surprises when you get home. You can determine, too, whether an olive has been around too long and has become soft when it should be crisp.

It is advisable to bring your own lidded jar with you so that you can store the olives in the mother brine. If you do purchase a carton of unbrined olives and plan to keep them for more than a few days, it would be best to make a brine or to add olive oil. Your olives can be kept out of the refrigerator in a cool place for a number of weeks. In fact, some importers claim that, properly kept in a salty brine in a cool place, olives can last upward of two years. Should you wish to store your olives out of the refrigerator, make sure they are totally submerged in brine. A harmless mold will form on the surface, which can be spooned off. Do not store your olives outside the refrigerator if you've added lemons or other perishable foods to the brine.

If certain olives are too strong for a dish you are planning to make with them, soak them in plain water for a few days or dunk them in boiling water for about ten minutes. The texture of green olives especially will not suffer from the brief boiling, although the color will change to brown-green. To bitter, dry-cured olives add oil, garlic, and herbs; these ingredients will help balance the strong olive flavor.

CALIFORNIA

DRY-CURED. Large for a dry-cured olive. Black and wrinkled. Dry-salt cured and rubbed with olive oil. Flavorful and meaty.

GREEK STYLE. Large, black-purple. Brine-cured and packed with vinegar. Size can vary. Fairly firm fleshed.

SICILIAN STYLE. Huge, medium green. Brine-cured and preserved with lactic acid, either added or produced by the olives themselves. Crisp. One variation is a cracked green that can be cured a shorter length of time. Spain exports a Sevillano that is similar.

CHILE

ALFONSO. Huge, pale purple to brown. Brine-cured, and too soft to be enjoyable.

FRANCE

GROSSANE. An unusual olive from southern France. Medium size, purple to black. Dry-cured, then soaked in a black pepper-flavored marinade.

NIÇOISE. Tiny, brown to brown-green-black. Brine-cured. High pit-to-meat ratio. Often packed with herbs, stems intact.

NYONS. Small, black, with green tint. Dry-salt-cured, then rubbed with olive oil. Rather bitter. There are brine-cured olives from Nyons as well.

PICHOLINE. Elongate, medium green and smooth. Salt-brine-cured. Sometimes lightly cured in lye. Bland, lightly salty. Sometimes packed with citric acid as a preservative when bottled in the United States.

GREECE

AMFISSA. Or Amphissa. Large-sized, purple to black. Brine-cured, with a full fruity flavor.

ATALANTI. Medium-large, dark green. Brine-cured, with a full flavor. Soft meat.

 **ELITSES.** Very small, ripe, dark brown-green. Firm-fleshed. Brine-cured. Surprisingly high meat to seed ratio. Sweet, delicate flavor.

 **IONIAN.** Medium-large, bright green. Brine-cured, firm textured with a buttery flavor.

 **KALAMATA.** Or Calamata. Medium size, black-purple. Slit, then brine-cured and packed with vinegar. Size can vary. A lovely, almond-shaped standby, appreciated by many.

 **NAFLION.** Or various other spellings. Medium size, dark green, cracked. Brine-cured, then packed with olive oil. Crisp, with a pleasant, youthful bite.

 **ROYAL.** Or Royal Victoria. Huge, red, dark brown, light brown from same batch. Slit, then salt-brine-cured and packed with vinegar and olive oil. Similar in flavor to the Kalamata. Size varies considerably. Often shipped in bulk and packed in bottles by the importer.

 SALONA. Round, medium size, brown to brownish-purple. Salt-brine-cured. Soft to mushy texture, salty but pleasing flavor. Small pit.

ISRAEL

SOURI. Small, pale olive. Brine-cured. Delicate in flavor.

ITALY

ASCOLANE. Very large, bright green olive from central Italy. Gentle flavors, a bit salty.

GAETA. Small, black and wrinkled. Dry-salt-cured, then rubbed with olive oil. Surprisingly mild. Other olives bearing this name are brine-cured.

LIGURIA. Small, black to brown-black. Salt-brine-cured. Cured for eight months. Tasty, alive. Sometimes packed with stems. Very slightly acidic.

LUGANO. Small, elongated, deep purple-black. Brine-cured. Rather salty. Sometimes packed with a few small olive leaves. A popular olive at tastings.

PONENTINE. Tiny, purple-black. Brine-cured, then packed with vinegar. Mild flavored.

MOROCCO

DRY-CURED. Large, black and wrinkled. Dry-salt-cured. Meaty. Bitter.

MOROCCO. The only name I know for this olive, although there are hundreds of different kinds of olives in Morocco, including a commonly seen dry-cured variety. Small, round, black-red to black. Brine-cured. Packed with twigs and leaves. Fairly firm-fleshed for such a large ripe olive.

SPAIN

ARBEQUIÑA. Tiny, round, pale green. Brine-cured. Firm and delicately flavored. Sold charmingly with olive leaves.

GORDAL. Large, green. Brine-cured.

Recipes

All the recipes compiled here have either olives or olive oil as a major ingredient. The recipes are Mediterranean in flavor, using not only olive oil as the chief cooking medium, but also the flavors that characterize Spanish, French, Italian and Greek cuisines: garlic, arugula, radicchio, goat and sheep cheeses, and such fresh aromatic herbs as oregano, basil, and rosemary.

The chef at Oliveto keeps a larder replete with fresh spices and many different olive oils from mild to fruity to peppery. The walk-in refrigerator is stocked with the freshest produce of the season. Finding conscientiously run stores that supply local produce from farmers who practice sustainable farming is the most important step to cooking fine feasts for friends who appreciate the culinary joys of life. For a more detailed description of key ingredients please see About the Ingredients page 177.

CURING
YOUR OWN

ALL VARIETIES OF FRESH, UNCURED OLIVES, AT ALL STAGES of ripeness, are inedible. Taste one and you will realize what a miracle the cured olive is. Curing leaches the bitter glucosides from the fruit's flesh. Lye treatments (old farming communities around the Mediterranean use ash) do the job most thoroughly, producing in just a few days fruit so bland that it must be doctored with salt, and sometimes herbs and other seasonings, for flavor. Water or brine treatments produce the tangy olives of the type most frequently imported in bulk—whether they be cracked greens, purple Kalamatas, or tiny Niçoises—and take anywhere from ten days (in the case of small cracked or needle-pricked olives) to three months (in the case of large, whole black olives) to leach out the bitterness. Some olives are aged in brine as long as eight months.

Making your own home-cured olives offers the same satisfaction as putting up any fruit or vegetable. Unfortunately, it is difficult to obtain fresh olives. In grocery stores in most parts of the United States—even in California, where 99 percent of the nation's commercial olive acreage is found—fresh olives, at any stage of ripeness, are a rarity. In urban markets, I have yet to see more than one variety offered at a time. In northern California, Mission olives (a fruity, oily but small variety) have found their way into certain vegetable markets. In other parts of the state, Manzanillos (the state's most commonly grown olive and one that is somewhat larger than the Mission) might be more commonly seen because they are the most widely grown variety in the Central Valley. A small quantity of Barounis is shipped to the East Coast for home pickling, where traditionalists who still pickle their own olives are numerous enough to warrant the transcontinental trip.

When a choice is possible, use the smaller olive; the huge Sevillano, the country's largest olive variety, has a low oil content and is less tasty than even the slightly smaller Ascolano. If you know of a store or farmers' market that sells fresh olives, you are in luck; beware of damaged olives, however, especially ripe ones. Often they are culls or have been so bruised in handling that they will produce a sorry pickled olive.

If you are in an olive-producing area, or have a friend or neighbor with a producing tree, or own one yourself, there is no style of cured olive you won't be able to produce, size being the only limitation. You will be able to pick olives at all stages of ripeness, carefully, one by one, and pickle them immediately. Especially when the olives are black (as in making the salt-cured type) and red (as in the Greek-style recipe), they are best just picked. Pickle the olives as soon after they are harvested as possible; bruises start to show up shortly after picking.

On the subject of making your own olive oil: Home economists are never at a loss for projects that take a long time, are messy, and produce ghastly results. Such projects, like the one for making olive oil at home, are on a par with a Girl Scout project I did as a child, making centerpieces out of pine cones, pipe cleaners, and Styrofoam balls. You can make your own olive oil with an automobile jack and boards rigged up as an improvised press. Good advice: Buy your olive oil. There is a reason good olive oil costs as much as it does, and it goes beyond labor costs.

Anzonini's Water-cured Green Olives

This recipe was given to me by a Spanish gypsy; it is almost identical to the method for making the pungent green olives of Provence called *olives cassées*. To make a more interesting mixture, add a few store-bought Kalamata olives to the jar several days before you plan on first serving them.

>   **5 pounds green mature olives**
>   **6 cups water**
>   **3 tablespoons salt**
>   **2 lemons, cut into ½-inch cubes**
>   **2 tablespoons dried oregano**
>   **2 cups white wine vinegar**
>   **6 cloves garlic, halved**
>   **2 tablespoons cumin seeds, crushed in a mortar**
>   **Olive oil**

Crack the flesh of the olives with a rolling pin, or by hitting each one individually with a hammer, but not so the flesh pulls away from the pit. Rinse with cold water. Place them in a stoneware, earthenware, glass, or porcelain jar and add cold water to cover. Weight the olives with a piece of wood or a plastic bag filled with water (to keep them submerged) and store in a dark, cool place for 10 days, changing the water every day.

Bring the water to a boil and dissolve the salt in it. Remove from the heat and let cool to room temperatures. Empty the liquid from the jar in which the olives have been soaking and discard it; rinse the olives in cold water and cover the olives with the cooled salt brine. Mix in the lemons, oregano, vinegar, garlic, and cumin seeds. Float enough olive oil on top to cover the surface.

Store in a cool place, even your refrigerator if you've the room, for at least 2 weeks, then leave them in your refrigerator or place in a cool cellar. The olives keep quite well for at least 2 months.

Makes about 5 pints.

Salt-cured Ripe Olives

These flavorful, if bitter, shriveled dry-cured olives—sometimes called oil-cured—will not keep nearly as well as brine-cured olives. Because of that and the fact that they are so pungent and not to everybody's liking, you might want to make only a small quantity of them. Use olives that are black or almost black. Mission olives are the best because of their high oil content and small size. Extra-large olives, such as the Sevillano, become soft.

Cover the bottom of a thick cardboard or wooden box with burlap or cheesecloth. In the box, mix together equal weights of noniodized salt and olives. Spread out evenly; then pour a layer of noniodized salt over the olives so that nearly all of them are covered, using an additional pound or so of salt. Place the box outdoors in the shade or in a basement so any liquid that oozes from it will not stain a floor or decking.

Stir the salt-covered olives well with a wooden spoon once a week for 4 weeks, or until the olives are cured. They should be slightly bitter.

Remove the olives from the salt by hand (unfortunately, I have found no better method). Bring a large pot of water to a rapid boil. Dip the olives into the boiling water for a few seconds, then drain in a colander and refresh with cold water. Spread the olives out on paper towels and let them dry for a few hours or overnight. Those olives you wish to eat within a few days should be coated with fruity olive oil (rub them with your fingers to distribute the oil), mixed with your favorite herbs, and kept in the refrigerator in a tightly capped jar. The remainder of the olives should be mixed at a ratio by weight of two parts olives to one part noniodized salt in a large glass jar or glazed pot, and kept in a cool place or refrigerated. They do not keep for more than a month.

Greek-Style Ripe Olives

For this recipe, choose olives that are red to dark red. Using a very sharp stainless-steel knife to reduce bruising, slash each olive deeply on one side. Place the olives in a large stoneware, earthenware, glass, or porcelain container. Make a solution of 1/4 cup salt dissolved in 1 quart water, and pour enough of the solution over the olives to immerse them. Weight the olives with a piece of wood or a plastic bag filled with water to submerge them completely. Store in a cool place, changing the solution once a week, for three weeks. If a scum forms on the surface during that time, disregard it until it is time to change the brine; then remove the scum and rinse the olives with fresh water before covering with brine again. The scum is harmless.

At the end of 3 weeks, taste one of the largest olives. If it is only slightly bitter (these olives should be left with a bit of a tang), pour off the brine and rinse the olives. If the olives are still quite bitter, rebrine them and soak for another week, then rinse. Using the following proportions, make enough marinade to cover the olives, putting them in the same large container you used for brining.

> **1 ½ cups white wine vinegar**
> **1 tablespoon salt dissolved in 2 cups water**
> **½ teaspoon dried oregano**
> **3 lemon wedges**
> **2 cloves garlic**

Pour the marinade over the olives and float enough olive oil to form a layer ¼-inch thick on top. The olives will be ready to eat after sitting in the marinade for just a few days. Store, still in the marinade, in a cool pantry or in the refrigerator. If kept too long, the lemon and vinegar flavors will predominate, so eat these within a month after they are ready.

Lye-cured Green Olives

On the street corners of Rome these sweet olives (*olive dolce*) are sold by the handful wrapped in paper cones for next to nothing. They last about a city block. They are a lovely, bright green color and are buttery in flavor. Use olives that are mature but still green, preferably the medium-sized Missions. Rinse the olives with water and place them in large glass or porcelain jars; then determine how much lye solution (see Note) you need to cover the amount of olives you have. Add a solution that has been mixed at the ratio of 1 quart water (at 65° to 70°F) to 1 tablespoon lye. Soak for 12 hours.

Drain the olives. Soak for 12 hours longer in a fresh batch of lye solution. Drain and rinse. Cut into the largest olive; if the lye has reached the pit, the lye cure is complete. (Usually two lye baths are enough for the small Mission olives seen in specialty produce stores. If one more bath is necessary, soak in fresh lye solution for 12 more hours, then drain and rinse with cold water.)

Soak the olives in fresh cold water, changing the water three (or more) times a day, for the next 3 days. At the end of 3 days, taste an olive to make sure there is no trace of lye flavor remaining.

Next, soak the olives for at least 1 day in a brine solution mixed at the ratio of 6 tablespoons salt to 1 gallon water. The olives are now ready for eating.

Store the olives in the brine solution in a cool, dark place, preferably the refrigerator. If you prefer a spicier flavor with a touch of vinegar, marinate them according to the recipe for Marinated Green or Green-Ripe Olives on page 72 and store in the refrigerator. Use within 2 months.

NOTE: Purchase lye in the "cleanser section" of your grocery store. Lye can cause serious burns. Keep lemon or vinegar handy to neutralize any that splashes onto your skin. If lye gets into your eyes, bathe them with running water and call your doctor. If it is swallowed, call your doctor, drink milk or egg white, and do not induce vomiting.

Marinated Black Olives

Some people would rather not bother with the canned California olive because it is so bland. Others appreciate it for its firm flesh, which is firm because it was picked green, whether it wound up green or black. This recipe and the one that follows give ways to add flavor to the unobtrusive, commercially prepared fruit, or extra dimensions to tastier brine-cured varieties. Using unpitted olives helps the aesthetic.

½ pound (about 2 cups) well-drained California black-ripe or other cured black olives
½ teaspoon dried oregano
½ teaspoon dried thyme
1 tablespoon coriander seeds, crushed in a mortar
2 bay leaves, broken in half
6 large pieces orange zest
¼ cup white wine vinegar
2 tablespoons salt dissolved in 2 cups water
Olive oil

In a jar just large enough to contain the olives and brine, layer the olives with the oregano, thyme, coriander, bay leaves, and orange zest so that the spices are well distributed among the olives. Add the vinegar, then pour in the salt brine to cover. Float enough olive oil on top to cover completely the surface of the liquid. Cover tightly and refrigerate for at least 1 week before eating.

Let the olives warm to room temperature before serving, so that the olive oil coats the olives as you remove them from the jar. Use within 1 month for best flavor.

Makes about 1 pint.

Marinated Green or Green-ripe Olives

The sweet olives described on page 70 can also be used with the following marinade. The California green-ripe olive is not a true ripe olive, but its curing and heating make it a pale green-brown instead of bright green.

> ½ pound (about 2 cups) green or California green-ripe olives
>   with their brine
> 1 large clove garlic, halved
> ½ teaspoon salt
> 1 dried red chili pepper
> ½ teaspoon oregano
> 2 bay leaves, broken in half
> ¼ cup white wine vinegar
> Olive oil

Pour off the olive brine and set aside. Put the olives in a jar they fill almost completely, interspersing the garlic, salt, chili pepper, oregano, and bay leaves among them. Add the vinegar. Mix enough of the reserved brine with an equal amount of water to fill the jar almost completely and pour the mixture into the jar. Float enough olive oil on top to cover completely the surface of the liquid. Cover tightly and refrigerate about 1 week before eating.

Let the olives warm to room temperature before serving, so that the olive oil coats the olives as you remove them from the jar. Use within a month for best flavor.

Makes about 1 pint.

FOR WHATEVER AILS YOU

Here is a list of ailments for which olive oil is an effective treatment, compiled from Mediterranean folklore and from nineteenth-century American medical practice:

Intestinal parasites "In cases of tapeworm," said Dr. Remondino, "olive oil often carried the gentleman, head, tail, and body, simply by its weight and volume."; bladder and kidney afflictions; inflammations of mucous membranes; simple diarrhea, dysentery, colic, flatulence, and constipation; the discomfort of teething; rheumatic diseases; yellow fever; tumors and diseases of the throat glands; and any disease resulting from poor assimilation of nutrients.

APPETIZERS

Feta, Garlic, and Olive Plate

If the olive is the fruit of the Mediterranean, surely garlic is the vegetable. One rarely finds the one flavor without the other. This pungent hors d'oeuvres plate was served to me by an aficionado of garlic—a man with passionate tastes in food—John Harris.

On a large platter, arrange over a bed of bitter greens (arugula, perhaps, with curly endive, cress, radicchio, or a combination) a layer of bite-size bits of creamy feta. Distribute whole cloves of garlic that have been gently stewed until soft in olive oil amidst the feta. Sprinkle fine olive oil over the cheese. Don't skimp. Sprinkle fresh herbs such as oregano or thyme over the cheese, as well as some finely chopped fresh Italian parsley and freshly ground black peppercorns. Garnish with Niçoise olives. (You might also garnish with sprigs of fresh thyme.) Serve with country-style bread, using the bread to soak up the oil.

Mozzarella Cheese Plate

Because fresh, whole-milk mozzarella is so delicate, it is a perfect vehicle for showing off your best olive oil—the olive oil with the most finesse.

Using the best mozzarella available, cut the cheese into the thinnest slices possible. (Do it with a wire cheese cutter when the cheese is cold.) Pour some delicate olive oil onto a serving platter. Rub both sides of the cheese slices in the oil and arrange the slices artfully on the platter. Serve surrounded by a variety of sweet ripe tomatoes in many colors, with still more olive oil sprinkled over all, and accompanied with a good bread. Give your guests a few options for additional flavors: a bit of freshly ground black peppercorns, a sprinkling of fresh thyme rubbed between the palms, a tad of coarse salt.

Mushrooms Stewed in Olive Oil

This simple hors d'oeuvre nicely complements a tray of cheese before dinner. It can also act as a garnish to add color and texture to a monotonous plate. Use plenty of freshly cracked black pepper; add just a few drops of lemon juice to cut down the oiliness.

> ½ **cup olive oil**
> **1 tablespoon coriander seeds, crushed in a mortar**
> **1 pound fresh wild mushrooms such as chanterelle, hedgehog,**
> **or morel, or any combination**
> **3 bay leaves, broken in half**
> **10 cherry tomatoes**
> **Fresh thyme, oregano, or marjoram sprigs**
> **Salt**
> **Freshly ground black pepper**
> **Lemon juice**

In a skillet over high heat, warm the olive oil. Add the coriander seeds and cook, stirring, for 2 minutes. Reduce the heat to medium, add the mushrooms and bay leaves and sauté until the mushrooms have stopped absorbing oil, at which point they are done. This should take about 8 minutes. At that moment, add the tomatoes and a few sprigs of thyme and cook for about 1 minute or so—not long enough to break the skins of the tomatoes.

Remove from the heat. Sprinkle with salt. Add plenty of pepper and a few drops of lemon juice. Allow to cool to room temperature before serving.

Serves 6.

Fried Chèvre

Warm chèvre, or goat cheese, is wonderful despite its stylishness. (Don't be deterred by columnists who have contempt for food chic.) I'll always remember when I first had warm chèvre (*chèvre chaud*—not speaking French, I thought I'd ordered the chef's show) on my maiden voyage to France. It was presented as a first course in an elegant Paris restaurant, served on a bed of bitter greens, dressed with a lemon vinaigrette. It is wonderful that way, or as the warming hors d'oeuvre described here.

> **14 oz. chèvre, without cinders, chilled**
> **1 egg**
> **1 tablespoon milk**
> **5 tablespoons toasted fine dried bread crumbs (see page 177)**
> **1½ teaspoons dried thyme**
> **½ baguette**
> **¼ cup olive oil, or more as needed**
> **1 clove garlic, minced, or more as needed**

Cut the chèvre into rounds ⅓-inch thick; you should have 8 rounds. In a small, shallow bowl, combine the egg and milk and beat together with a fork until blended. Stir together the bread crumbs and thyme in a separate bowl. Cut the baguette in half horizontally, then cut crosswise into pieces the size of the chèvre rounds. Place the bread on a platter.

Dip both sides of each chèvre slice in the egg mixture, then dredge in the bread crumb mixture. In a heavy skillet over high heat, warm ¼ cup olive oil and the garlic until the olive oil reaches the vapor stage (never let it smoke). Add 4 chèvre slices and cook, turning once gently with a spatula, 1 minute per side: be careful not to disturb the crust.

Place the hot cheese on the baguette pieces. Add more oil and garlic to the pan, if necessary, and cook the remaining 4 chèvre slices in the same way. Drizzle any oil and garlic remaining in the pan over the bread and cheese. Serve immediately.

Makes 8 large servings.

Tuna and Olive Antipasto

For years I have purchased this antipasto from my neighborhood delicatessen, a shop owned by Italians from Genoa. It is almost a pickle, and is not meant to be eaten alone. It is a fine accompaniment on a picnic, and can be used as an antipasto with cured meats, squid salad, and Italian bread.

> 2 small boiling potatoes (such as yellow Finns), unpeeled, cubed
> 7 tablespoons olive oil
> 1 yellow onion, thinly sliced
> 1 clove garlic, minced
> 6 tomatoes, peeled, seeded, and chopped, with their juice
> 2 bay leaves
> ½ teaspoon dried oregano
> 2 carrots, peeled and thickly sliced
> 3 celery stalks, thickly sliced
> ½ pound tuna fillet
> 1 can (6 ounces) tomato paste, or, preferably, ¾ cup homemade tomato paste (see page 181)
> 2 tablespoons chopped capers
> ¼ cup white wine vinegar
> Hot-pepper flakes
> 6 anchovy fillets, rinsed and torn into pieces
> ¼ to ⅓ pound small, black brine-cured olives such as Niçoise
> Salt

Arrange the potatoes on a steamer rack over boiling water, cover the pan, and steam until just tender, about 15 minutes.

Preheat a broiler. Meanwhile, heat 2 tablespoons of the olive oil in a sauce-pan. Add the onion and garlic and sauté until soft, about 5 minutes. Next add the tomatoes and their liquid, bay leaves, oregano, and carrots; cover and simmer for 5 minutes. Add the celery, re-cover, and simmer until the vegetables are tender but crisp, about 5 minutes more.

While the vegetables are cooking, rub the tuna on both sides with 2 table-spoons of the olive oil and place on a broiler pan. Broil on both sides, turning once, until done (the tuna should still be barely pink inside), about 5 minutes on each side. Break up the tuna into bite-size pieces.

Remove the vegetables from the heat and add the tomato paste, capers, vinegar, a good sprinkling of hot-pepper flakes, the tuna, anchovies, olives, potatoes, and the remaining 3 tablespoons olive oil. Stir gently until just mixed. Season with salt to taste. Let cool, cover, and refrigerate.

Serve at room temperature or slightly chilled.

Serves 8.

Olive-and-Anchovy Stuffed Eggs

Deviled eggs are comforting; they make me think of simpler times and my old green lunch box. The following recipe for stuffed eggs would, no doubt, have little appeal for children. It is for a more mature palate.

> **Olive oil for sautéing**
> **10 cloves garlic**
> **2 anchovy fillets, rinsed**
> **5 hard-cooked eggs (see page 179)**
> **2 teaspoons capers, minced**
> **2½ tablespoons fine olive oil**
> **1 tablespoon white wine vinegar**
> **¼ cup Sicilian-style green olives, pitted and minced**
> **1 heaping tablespoon finely chopped fresh cilantro**
> **Large pinch of cayenne pepper**
> **Paper-thin purple onion slices**

In a skillet over medium heat, warm a little olive oil. Add the garlic cloves and sauté, until just golden, about 5 minutes. Remove from the heat and transfer to a small bowl; let cool.

Add the anchovy fillets to the garlic and, using a fork, mash together well. Halve the eggs lengthwise and scoop the yolks into the anchovy mixture. Mash thoroughly. Mix in the capers. Slowly add the fine olive oil while continuing to stir with a fork. Stir in the wine vinegar, olives, cilantro, and cayenne pepper, mixing well.

Cut a sliver from the bottom of each egg half so it will not tip. Using a spoon mound the yolk mixture in the egg halves. Garnish with bits of purple onion and serve.

Makes 10 stuffed eggs.

Tapénade

Although its origin is Provence, *tapénade*, which is basically a black olive paste, has been made in many places in many ways. It has so many uses that the variations are justified. It can be spread on crackers, *crostini* (see page 88), or bread; used between layers in pastry or filo dough; indulged in as a dip for vegetables; or used atop a piece of grilled salmon. Here are three diverse recipes.

Simple Tapénade

Serve this very pungent *tapénade* with lightly parboiled or raw vegetables such as fennel bulbs, green onions, cauliflower, carrots, or broccoli, or with cooked artichoke leaves. Or try it on unsalted *crostini* (see page 88).

4 anchovy fillets, rinsed
½ cup pitted Kalamata olives
2 tablespoons capers, minced
¼ cup olive oil
1 tablespoon Dijon mustard

In a blender, food processor, or mortar, combine the anchovies, olives, capers, olive oil, and mustard. Blend or grind with a pestle until thoroughly mixed. If the *tapénade* is too thick, drizzle more olive oil into the mixture as you continue to blend (or grind with a pestle) for a bit longer.

Serves 6.

California Tapénade

Offer unsalted tortilla chips for dipping.

6 ounces (about 1 ½ cups) California pitted black-ripe olives
2 tablespoons capers
4 anchovy fillets, rinsed and chopped
3 tablespoons olive oil
2 large cloves garlic, minced
1 tablespoon bottled hot tomato or tomatillo salsa made with onions
½ teaspoon dried oregano
2 teaspoons fresh lime juice
3 tablespoons finely chopped yellow onion
Red-leaf lettuce or curly endive
¾ cup sour cream
1 lime, cut into wedges

In a blender or food processor, combine the olives, capers, anchovies, olive oil, garlic, salsa, oregano, and lime juice. Blend until smooth. Add the onion and blend briefly to mix.

To serve, line a shallow bowl with lettuce. Mound the *tapénade* in the center and top with the sour cream. Squeeze the juice from half of the lime wedges over all. Garnish with the lime wedges.

Serves 6.

Tuna Tapénade

"What do you guys think of this *tapénade*?" I ventured. "I don't usually like anchovies," said one friend, "but this is irresistible." "It's like a sardine sandwich in a drum—industrial-strength sardines," said one wise guy. This recipe is quite good, and makes a large quantity. If you make it ahead of time, stir before serving; the oil tends to separate. Serve with *crostini* (see page 88) or fresh vegetables.

> ½ **pound tuna fillet**
> ¼ **cup olive oil**
> ¼ **cup capers, rinsed and chopped**
> **5 anchovy fillets, rinsed and chopped**
> **1 cup brine-cured black olives, such as Kalamata, pitted**
> **3 large cloves garlic, chopped**
> **Freshly ground black pepper**
> **3 tablespoons brandy**
> **1 hard-cooked egg (page 179), grated**

Preheat a broiler. Rub the tuna on both sides with a few teaspoons of the olive oil and place on a broiler pan. Broil on both sides, turning once, and grill until just done (the tuna should still be fairly pink inside), about 5 minutes for each side. Tear it into small pieces with your fingers and set aside.

In a blender or food processor, combine the capers, anchovies, olives, garlic, pepper to taste, tuna, and brandy. Blend until mixed.

With the motor still running, slowly add the remaining olive oil and blend until the tapénade is smooth. It should have the consistency of mayonnaise. Garnish with the egg.

Serves 10 to 12.

Aioli

One of the loveliest, most festive meals I ever had was an *aioli monstre*, modeled after the town-wide garlic feasts held in Provençal villages. At a groaning table were parboiled, steamed, and raw vegetables of all varieties—fennel bulb, broccoli, new potatoes, lettuces, cherry tomatoes, mushrooms, asparagus, radishes, artichoke hearts, carrots, cauliflower, and so on—hard-cooked eggs, chunks of poached salmon, and thinly sliced rare beef. We dipped it all in a twelve-clove aioli, and drank a young Bordeaux. For three days afterward I smelled like Provence.

A light olive oil is most pleasing to the palate for this potent sauce; a gold rather than green oil is most pleasing to the eye. Start this recipe with three cloves of garlic, then taste. Add more mashed garlic, according to your preference and the strength of your garlic. If your garlic is old (sold after its prime), remove the green sprouts in the middle as they are bitter and they give a green cast to your aioli. A true aioli will have about eight garlic cloves for each cup of olive oil, but such a heavy-duty item is to few American chefs' taste. At Oliveto, we add about one fat clove per yolk, depending on the garlic season. Serve the sauce with the foods suggested above.

> **3 new cloves garlic**
> **3 egg yolks**
> **1½ cups mild fine olive oil such as a Provençal oil**
> **Fresh lemon juice to thin (about ½ lemon)**
> **Salt**
> **Freshly ground black pepper**

In a bowl with a curved bottom, or, better yet, in a heavy mortar (try to find one in an Asian market), mash the garlic cloves with a pestle. With a wire whisk (or with the pestle if you've a heavy, smooth mortar), whip the egg yolks with the garlic paste until it is a pale yellow, a few minutes. This step is most important. Now add the oil, drop by drop, continuing to whisk. After one-third of the oil is incorporated, thin the yolk mixture with the lemon juice. Then increase the rate of oil addition to a very fine drizzle, continuing to whisk all the while, until all the oil is incorporated. Season with salt and pepper to taste as the last of the oil is beaten in. The aioli will have the consistency of a thick mayonnaise. You should have about 1¾ cups.

Variations:

Add 2 tablespoons puréed sun-dried tomatoes to the finished aioli.

Use orange or blood-orange juice instead of lemon juice.

Omit the garlic cloves and add 2 tablespoons roasted garlic purée, chopped black olives to taste, and capers and anchovies to the finished aioli.

For a spicy remoulade to accompany a grilled fish, add a sprinkling of cayenne pepper; a sprinkling of celery seed; 1 shallot, minced; 1 stalk celery, minced; chopped fresh Italian parsley; capers, chopped to taste; and 6 to 8 cornichons, minced.

Marinated Chèvre

Simply marinated chèvre makes a delicious Provençal appetizer, and, while it marinates in the kitchen, it is as decorative as a vase of flowers. It is important to have a crusty bread on which to serve the cheese, one that will hold together when saturated with olive oil. Use small, round chèvres, such as a Lezay or those made by Laura Chenel's California chèvre, or slice a Montrachet log (without cinders) into five-ounce lengths and press the cut ends to prevent any disintegration.

> **1 or more pieces chèvre, 5 ounces each**
> **6 cloves garlic for each 5 ounces of cheese**
> **1 fresh thyme sprig, for each 5 ounces of cheese**
> **12 Niçoise olives (for each 5 ounces of cheese)**
> **Fine olive oil**
> **Crusty baguette or other crusty bread slices**

Place the cheese in a jar or glass that is only slightly larger in diameter than your cheese. Add the garlic cloves, thyme sprigs, and olives. If marinating more than 1 piece of cheese, scatter the garlic cloves, thyme sprigs, and olives between the cheeses. Pour in enough olive oil to cover the cheese, cover the jar, and allow to marinate in a cool place at least 2 days.

Serve the marinated cheese with the bread slices. Pour some of the marinating oil into a small bowl so that guests can spoon the oil over the bread before topping with the cheese. Serve the olives in their own small bowl. Any leftover oil can be used to dress the next day's salad or to sauté vegetables.

One 5-ounce piece of cheese serves 4.

Bagna Cauda

In Piedmontese dialect, *bagna cauda* means "hot bath" and is made there with cream rather than olive oil, reflecting the greater use of butter and cream in the cooking of the north than in that of central and southern Italy. *Bagna cauda* is customarily served warm over a flame with pieces of raw or parboiled vegetables—broccoli, green onions, cauliflower, fennel bulbs, carrots, romaine lettuce leaves, mushrooms, bell peppers, endives, asparagus tips, turnips, radishes—and breadsticks for dipping. Pungent and garlicky, it is not a dish for the timorous. Be sure to serve it before a meal it will not stifle.

4 cloves garlic
12 anchovy fillets, rinsed
3 slices toast, crusts removed
3 tablespoons heavy cream
1 cup fine olive oil
Freshly ground black pepper
2 tablespoons unsalted butter

In a wooden bowl, use a pestle to crush together the garlic and the anchovies until they form a paste. Soak the toast in the cream, crumble it into fine crumbs, and add it to the paste, continuing to mash with the pestle. While stirring with a fork or wire whisk, add the olive oil, little by little, until all of it is incorporated. Add a generous grinding of black pepper.

In a small saucepan over medium-low heat, melt the butter and stir in the anchovy mixture. Heat just until warm through. Transfer to a chafing dish or fondue pot over a flame and serve.

Serves 8.

CROSTINI

These crisp, mildly garlicky toasts have many uses. They are ideal accompaniments to antipasto platters or thick soups, or they can be topped with cannellini bean purée or a Tuscan chicken liver spread and served as an antipasto. It is wonderful to be able to make these versatile toasts yourself in just a few minutes. Cut a thick sourdough baguette into slices 1/3 inch thick. Brush both sides of each slice lightly with olive oil. Toast on a baking sheet at 350F until golden; you may have to turn them so both sides are equally crisp. Lightly rub top sides with a garlic clove while they are still warm.

Possible toppings include:

Thinly sliced Parmesan cheese (sliced with a vegetable peeler) drizzled with fine olive oil.

Olivade made by combining 1 cup (8 ounces) whole-milk ricotta; 1/2 pound (about 2 cups) brine-cured black olives (such as Niçoise or Ponentine), pitted and chopped; 1 tablespoon Cognac; and 1 tablespoon finely chopped sun-dried tomato.

A mild cheese melted atop the toast under the broiler, topped with mushrooms that have been thinly sliced and marinated in a vinaigrette.

Chicken livers sautéed in olive oil with onions, then crushed in a bowl with fine olive oil, minced fresh rosemary, salt, and freshly ground black pepper to taste. Garnish each *crostino* with a tiny sprig of rosemary.

FIRST COURSES

Carpaccio

An elegant but simple first course that is a fine way to enjoy the best olive oil and the best beef. The unassertive raw beef will not compete with the oil, and the capers will heighten its flavor. Many restaurants freeze the beef before they cut it in order to produce the thinnest slice possible. Freezing does compromise the flavor of good beef, however. The beef tastes much better sliced a little thicker and then pounded as thin as possible.

2 ounces lean beef fillet per serving, thinly sliced
2 fresh mushrooms per serving, thinly sliced with a vegetable
  peeler
1 teaspoon capers per serving
1 lemon wedge per serving
Fine olive oil
Freshly ground black pepper

Multiply the ingredient amounts according to the number of diners. Place each beef slice between two pieces of waxed paper. Using the flat side of a meat pounder or a broad, heavy knife, pound the beef until it is of a thin, even thickness.

To serve, arrange the beef on large, chilled serving plates. Garnish each serving with the mushroom slices, capers, and a lemon wedge. Pass the oil in a cruet, letting each guest drizzle it over the beef to taste. Hide the salt shakers for this course, but do pass the peppermill.

Egg Pasta

Many Italians maintain that fresh egg pasta should be served with cream and butter sauces, whereas oil and tomato sauces are best with first-rate packaged dried pasta. The following is a good, basic pasta recipe that can be served fresh after it is cut, as described here, or dried. I use a hand-cranked pasta machine to make the noodles. Should you buy your noodles fresh, make sure they have been rolled and cut, not extruded.

> **1½ cups all-purpose flour, plus flour for dusting**
> **1 egg**
> **1 egg white**
> **1 tablespoon olive oil**
> **1 teaspoon salt**

Put the 1½ cups flour in a mixing bowl and make a well in the center. Put the egg, egg white, olive oil, and salt in the well. With a fork, pull the walls of flour into the well, blending together all the ingredients. Using your fingers, form the mixture into a ball. Add a little water to incorporate any remaining flour that will not stick to the dough, but keep the dough as dry as possible.

Knead the dough on a floured board until it is shiny and elastic, about 10 minutes. Cut the dough into thirds and wrap each portion in waxed paper. Let rest for 10 minutes.

Start with the pasta machine at the number 1 setting. Dust a portion of the dough with plenty of flour to keep it from sticking and flatten it between your palms. Repeat the feeding of the dough through the rollers, changing the setting each time. Run it through the roller. Then run the dough through the machine once again at the same setting. Continue in this manner, running the dough through each of the lower settings twice until the pasta dough is as thin as you want it. Then dust it with flour and set it aside on a cotton tea towel. (You may have to use several towels as the pasta sheets can be very long.) Repeat with the remaining 2 dough portions, stacking the pasta sheets one on top of the other with plenty of flour between them.

Set the cutter at the desired width and run each pasta sheet through the machine. Set the noodles aside, dusted with plenty of flour. Bring a large pot filled with salted water to a rapid boil. Drop in the pasta and stir once with a fork immediately after it is in the water. Boil for a very short time—as little as half a minute for the thinnest of pasta—until al dente. Drain in a colander and use as directed in individual recipes.

Serves 4 as a first course or 3 as a main course.

Pasta with Cream, Feta, Olives, and Basil

Surprisingly, this rich first-course dish only starts the juices flowing. It should be followed by a light main course. Fresh basil is important to offset the salty feta and olives; dried basil must not be substituted. The basil and olives are added at the last minute so they will not discolor the sauce.

> **1 recipe Egg Pasta dough (see page 92), very thinly rolled**
> **1 cup heavy cream**
> **¼ pound feta cheese, crumbled**
> **Salt**
> **⅓ cup dry-cured black olives, pitted and cut into small pieces**
> **⅔ cup finely chopped fresh basil**
> **Cracked black peppercorns**

Prepare the pasta dough and run the sheets through the cutters on the pasta machine at the desired noodle width. Set aside, dusting the strands with plenty of flour so they do not stick together.

Put a large pot filled with salted water over high heat and bring to a boil. Meanwhile, in a wide skillet over medium heat, reduce the cream by about one fourth; add the feta. Stir until the feta is somewhat melted but the sauce is still lumpy.

Add the noodles to the boiling water and cook as directed on page 93. Drain in a colander, then transfer the noodles to the skillet. Add the olives, basil, and peppercorns. Using tongs, toss to distribute the sauce. Transfer to a warmed platter or individual plates and serve immediately.

Serves 4.

Pasta with Shrimp and Picholines

A delicate dish in spite of the heavy cream. The colors are pastels, the flavors refined. It is very nice with a crisp California Sauvignon Blanc, a white Burgundy, or a Sancerres.

Salt
4 tomatoes, peeled, seeded, and diced
2 recipes Egg Pasta dough (see page 92), thinly rolled
1 tablespoon unsalted butter
2 cloves garlic, minced
Grated zest of 1 lemon
1½ pounds shrimp, peeled and deveined
1½ cups heavy cream
1 bunch fresh tarragon, stemmed and chopped
1 cup Picholine olives, pitted and cut into pieces

Lightly salt the tomatoes and set aside in a colander to drain.

Meanwhile, prepare the pasta dough and run the sheets through the cutters on the pasta machine at the desired noodle width. Set aside, dusting the strands with plenty of flour so they do not stick together.

In a large (5-quart) pot over medium-high heat, melt the butter. Add the garlic and sauté until lightly browned, about 5 minutes. Add the lemon zest, shrimp, and drained tomatoes. Cover and cook for a few minutes until the shrimp have just changed color. Remove the shrimp and set aside; keep warm. Drain off the excess liquid. Add the cream to the pan and reduce the sauce over medium heat by one third. Keep warm.

Cook the pasta as directed in the recipe, considerably less than 1 minute. Drain in a colander and add to the sauce along with the shrimp, tarragon, and olives. Season with salt to taste, and, using tongs, toss to distribute the sauce.

Transfer to a warmed platter or individual plates and serve immediately.

Serves 8.

Pasta with Julie's Puttanesca Sauce

Two stories: prostitutes cook up this fragrant sauce to lure customers to their door; wives who spend their afternoons engrossed with *innamorati* can prepare this delicious dish quickly, keeping their husbands satisfied and unsuspecting.

> **Salt**
> **4 large tomatoes, peeled, seeded, and diced (about 3 cups)**
> **¼ cup olive oil**
> **2 small dried red chili peppers, minced**
> **4 large cloves garlic, minced**
> **6 anchovy fillets, rinsed and chopped**
> **2 cups sliced, pitted Kalamata olives**
> **¼ cup capers, rinsed and chopped**
> **1 pound dried pasta such as fettuccine or the like**
> **Chopped fresh Italian parsley**

Lightly salt the tomatoes and set aside in a colander to drain.

Meanwhile, in a skillet over medium-high heat, warm the olive oil. Add the chili peppers and sauté for 1 minute. Add the garlic and sauté for 1 minute longer. Add the anchovies, drained tomatoes, olives, and capers. Season with salt to taste. Stir well and simmer, uncovered, for 10 minutes.

Meanwhile, bring a large pot filled with salted water to a rapid boil. Add the pasta and cook until al dente; the timing depends on the pasta brand and the size and shape of the noodles. Drain in a colander and divide among 4 warmed individual plates.

Spoon the sauce atop the pasta, sprinkle with parsley, and serve immediately.

Serves 4.

Pasta al Pesto

Pesto is a versatile summer standby. It can be used to dress a simple pasta, added as a dollop in a hearty minestrone, mixed into aioli, and so on. Freeze it in small quantities to use in making a quick meal.

2 cups firmly packed fresh basil leaves
1 teaspoon salt
4 cloves garlic, minced
3 tablespoons pine nuts, toasted
1 ½ cups fine olive oil
Freshly ground black pepper
½ cup freshly grated parmigiano-reggiano cheese
1 ½ pounds dried linguini

Chop the basil. Place the salt and garlic in a mortar. Add the basil little by little, and, using a pestle, crush it with the salt and garlic until it forms a paste. Begin adding the olive oil slowly, alternating with the pine nuts and continuing to work the mixture with the pestle. Add a bit of pepper as well, as you continue making a paste of all the ingredients except the cheese.

When you have finished, the mixture should still be a paste. Add the cheese and incorporate with the pestle. You should have about 1 ½ cups.

Bring a large pot filled with salted water to a rapid boil. Add the pasta and cook until al dente; the timing depends on the pasta brand and the size and shape of the noodles. Drain in a colander and return to the pot. Toss with the pesto to taste.

Serves 6.

Polenta

Polenta is a staple at Oliveto. It is endlessly versatile, appropriate fresh from the pot as a complement to sautéed meats or to braised dishes such as Daube Beef, (see page 124, without the potatoes), or Lamb Shanks with Feta, Red Bell Peppers, and Olives (see page 122), or as a base for rich sauces such as the sausage and mushroom sauce on page 101. It can also be broiled, fried in olive oil, or grilled over a hot charcoal fire, and served as an as an accompaniment to almost any hearty main course that comes to mind. Plus, for a morning cereal, there is nothing quite as good as a bowl of hot polenta with honey and light cream.

> **8 cups water, for soft polenta, or 6 cups water, for polenta for grilling or frying**
> **2 teaspoons salt**
> **2 cups polenta (coarse cornmeal)**
> **Olive oil for frying or grilling**

In a large pot, bring the water and salt to a boil. Very slowly add the polenta while stirring constantly with a wooden spoon. Cook, stirring all the while, until the polenta comes away from the sides of the pot, at least 45 minutes.

If the polenta is to be served soft, serve it immediately. If it is to be served grilled or fried, turn it out onto a sheet pan (no need to grease the pan) and smooth the top. Let cool and then cut into triangles for grilling or frying.

To fry the polenta, use a cast-iron skillet over high heat, pour in olive oil to a depth of ½ inch. Heat to the vapor stage. Slip the polenta pieces into the hot oil and fry, turning once, until golden brown, about 3 minutes on each side.

Preheat a broiler. To broil the polenta pieces, brush both sides lightly with olive oil and place on a broiler pan. Broil the polenta about 4 inches from the heat source until browned on the first side. Turn and broil until a golden brown on the second side, about 3 minutes. To grill the polenta pieces, brush them lightly with oil and place on a grill rack over charcoal; the timing is about the same as for broiling. Serve hot.

Serves 10 to 12.

Winter Polentas

During the winter, these polentas are good with the dishes noted in the introduction to the basic polenta recipe on page 98.

Bake 4 large sweet potatoes (poke before roasting) until tender in a 425°F oven for about 45 minutes, then peel and mash them. Stir the hot mashed sweet potatoes into the soft polenta just before serving.

Peel and then boil in cream (not milk, as it will separate) 1 large or 2 or 3 small celery roots until they are soft. Purée them in a food mill or food processor, then stir into the soft polenta just before serving.

Pasta with Olive Oil and Garlic

Heat 2 tablespoons olive oil in a skillet over medium heat. Add 10 cloves garlic, minced, and sauté until they are crisp and light brown, about 5 minutes. Meanwhile, bring a large pot of water to a boil, salt the water, and add 1 pound dried pasta. (I prefer spaghettini for this dish.) Cook until al dente; timing will depend on size and shape of pasta and the brand. Drain well in a colander. Return to the pot and toss with the garlic pieces and 1/3 to 1/2 cup fine olive oil; add salt to taste and a good sprinkling of freshly ground black pepper. Serves 4 for a first course.

Risotto

Risotto is a rich first course typical of northern Italian meals. Served with meat sauces or with shellfish or vegetables mixed in, it can even be offered as a main course. It is also a perfect vehicle for wild mushrooms and truffles or other prized, fragrant seasonal items; and, perhaps most important for this volume, it is a wonderful way to taste the finest olive oils.

Risotto is usually made with Arborio rice, which is grown in the Po Valley in Piedmont and has a white fleck at the center of each kernel (see About the Ingredients, page 177). Do not expect a light, fluffy rice. A good risotto is very rich and must be cooked al dente with kernels that adhere to one another in a rich "cream."

> 3 cups full-flavored chicken stock
> 1 large yellow onion, finely chopped
> 4 tablespoons unsalted butter
> ¼ cup olive oil
> 1⅓ cups Arborio rice (superfino)
> ⅓ cup tightly packed freshly grated parmigiano-reggiano cheese
> Freshly ground black pepper
> A cruet of Tuscan fine olive oil

Pour the chicken stock into a saucepan and bring to a simmer. Meanwhile, in a heavy saucepan over medium heat, melt the butter with the oil. Add the onion and sauté until golden, about 5 minutes. Add the rice and mix well with a wooden spoon until the rice is well coated with butter and oil. Using a ladle, add about ½ cup stock, then stir the rice constantly until the stock is absorbed. Immediately add about ½ cup of the stock and continue to cook and stir until the stock is absorbed. Continue in the same manner, always waiting until the rice has absorbed all the stock before adding more. When all the stock has been added in this manner, the rice should be al dente. If the rice is too chewy, add more stock and stir to incorporate. A proper risotto takes a little patience, and constant stirring.

Remove from the heat, stir in the cheese, and season with pepper to taste. Serve in individual bowls with fine olive oil for pouring over the top.

Serves 4.

Sausage and Mushroom Sauce

This rich, fragrant sauce is delicious spooned over a plate of hot soft polenta (see page 98) or a creamy risotto (see page 100). Use any dried mushrooms you wish; even inexpensive ones will work well.

> ½ cup dried mushrooms
> 2 tablespoons plus ½ cup fine olive oil
> 4 small sweet Italian sausages
> 3 cloves garlic, minced
> 3 large tomatoes, peeled and seeded
> Hot-pepper flakes

Place the mushrooms in a bowl and add warm water to cover. Let stand for about 1 hour to soften thoroughly.

Drain the mushrooms, squeeze out the excess water, and slice. Set aside. In a skillet, over medium-high heat, warm the 2 tablespoons oil. Add the sausages and garlic and sauté until the sausages are almost done. Add the tomatoes and, stirring frequently, sauté until the tomatoes are cooked, about 5 minutes.

Remove the sausages from the skillet, cut them into bite-size pieces, and then return them to the pan. Add the reserved mushrooms, and pour in the ½ cup oil. Season with the hot-pepper flakes to taste. Place over low heat and, stirring constantly, heat to warm the sauce through; be careful not to cook the oil as cooking changes its flavor. Serve very hot.

Serves 4.

SOUPS

Gazpacho

I first had this memorable pink gazpacho made with cream years ago in Barcelona. Its flavors are so pronounced that it creates the dilemma of what to serve for a second course. It is difficult to find a better follow-up than a simple grill.

½ red bell pepper, seeded and cut up
1 white onion, coarsely chopped
1 clove garlic, minced
4 tomatoes, peeled, seeded, and coarsely chopped
1 celery heart, coarsely chopped
1 cup heavy cream
2 cups chicken stock
2 teaspoons salt
¼ cup rice vinegar
¾ cup fine olive oil
5 dashes Tabasco sauce, or to taste
1 cucumber, peeled, seeded, and cut into small cubes
Fresh cilantro leaves

In a food processor, combine the bell pepper, onion, garlic, tomatoes, celery heart, cream, chicken stock, salt, vinegar, ½ cup of the olive oil, and the Tabasco sauce. (This may have to be done in batches, depending on the capacity of your machine.) Purée the mixture. The soup should be somewhat smooth.

Transfer to a large bowl, cover, and refrigerate until nicely cooled. Ladle into individual bowls and garnish each bowl with cucumber, a drizzling of the remaining 1/4 cup olive oil, and cilantro leaves.

Serves 6.

Pappa al Pomodoro

"You've got to have a recipe for *pappa al pomodoro*," my Tuscan friend insisted. And so I do. The rustic tomato-and-bread dish should be accompanied with plenty of good olive oil at the table to pour over it. It has the consistency of pudding, and it is also wonderful offered as the main course of a simple lunch.

> ⅓ cup olive oil
> 6 cloves garlic, minced
> Hot-pepper flakes
> 2 pounds ripe tomatoes, peeled, seeded, and chopped
> 1½ pounds day-old, dry crusty whole-wheat or white bread, torn into 1½-inch pieces
> 4½ cups chicken stock
> Leaves from 1 bunch fresh basil
> Salt
> A cruet of fine olive oil

In a 5-quart pot over medium-high heat, warm the olive oil. Add the garlic and a hearty shake of hot-pepper flakes and sauté until the garlic is golden, about 5 minutes. Add the tomatoes and simmer uncovered, stirring occasionally, for 15 minutes. Add the bread, chicken stock, basil leaves, and salt. Stir very well, so all the liquid is absorbed by the bread, then cover and simmer over low heat for 10 minutes, to blend the flavors. Turn off the heat and let rest for 1 hour.

Just before serving, reheat gently to prevent scorching. Serve with fine olive oil at the table.

Serves 8.

Bean Soup from Tuscany

This delicious wintertime soup is easy to make, and goes nicely with any coarse, country-style bread.

1 pound (about 2¼ cups) dried small white beans
2 quarts light chicken stock
4 bay leaves
2 teaspoons dried oregano
6 tablespoons olive oil
2 teaspoons salt
¼ cup finely chopped fresh Italian parsley
4 cloves garlic, minced
5 tablespoons fresh lemon juice
A cruet of Tuscan fine olive oil

Rinse the beans and place in a saucepan with water to cover. Bring to a boil, then remove from heat, cover, and let stand for 1 hour. Drain the beans. In a large heavy-bottomed pot, combine the beans, chicken stock, bay leaves, oregano, and the olive oil. Bring to a boil, cover, reduce the heat to medium-low, and simmer until the beans are tender, about 1 hour. Remove and discard the bay leaves.

Add the salt. Remove half of the beans and their liquid and place in a food processor. Process to form a purée. Return the puréed beans to the pot. Add the parsley, garlic, and lemon juice and simmer for 10 minutes.

To serve, ladle into large individual soup bowls. Encourage your guests to add the fine olive oil liberally.

Serves 4 to 6.

Minestrone from Chianti, Country Style

For the best flavor, serve this Tuscan soup the day after it is made. If you want to skip the first day's version altogether, simply put two thick slices of bread into the pot of soup before it is refrigerated; they will thicken the soup nicely. The next day's version, *ribollita* ("reboiled"), should be heated until just simmering. The olive oil (preferably a Tuscan one) and freshly grated parmigiano-reggiano garnishes are essential both days.

½ cup dried small white beans
5 cups water
1 large ham hock
¼ cup olive oil
⅓ bunch celery, chopped
1 potato, diced
1 yellow onion, thinly sliced
1 bunch fresh Italian parsley, minced
1 carrot, peeled and sliced
6 cloves garlic, minced
1 head Savoy cabbage, coarsely chopped
1 bunch kale or collard greens, coarsely chopped
3 large tomatoes, peeled, seeded, and coarsely chopped
Salt
Freshly ground black pepper
1 loaf country-style bread, thickly sliced
Freshly grated parmigiano-reggiano cheese
A cruet of fine olive oil

Rinse the beans and place in a saucepan with water to cover. Bring to a boil then remove from the heat, cover, and let stand for 1 hour. Drain the beans and return them to the pan. Add the 5 cups water and the ham hock. Bring to a simmer, cover and cook until the beans are just tender, about 1 hour. Remove from the heat and set aside.

In a large pot over medium-high heat, warm the olive oil. Add the celery, potato, onion, most of the parsley, carrot, and garlic. Sauté, stirring often, until the vegetables are just beginning to soften, about 10 minutes. Stir in the cabbage, kale, and tomatoes.

Meanwhile, remove the ham hock from the beans. Remove the skin and discard, then cut the meat from the bone in bite-size pieces. Add both the meat and the bone to the pot. Using a slotted spoon, remove half the beans from their liquid and set aside. With a potato masher, mash the rest of the beans with their liquid and add to the pot holding the vegetables.

Cover and simmer for 15 minutes. Add water to cover (about 6 cups), re-cover, and simmer for 30 minutes. Add the whole beans and season to taste with salt and pepper; the amount will depend on the saltiness of the ham.

If you are serving the soup the day it is made, put a bread slice at the bottom of a large tureen. Add a few ladlesful of soup, then another layer of thick bread, and then another few ladlesful of soup. Continue in this manner until the tureen is full, ending with the soup. Sprinkle the cheese and the reserved parsley on top. Cover and let stand for 10 minutes.

Serve in large bowls. Have fine olive oil and more cheese handy at the table. Do not scrimp when pouring the olive oil into the bowls.

Serves 6.

Olive and Chick-Pea Soup

At Oliveto, chick-peas (a.k.a. garbanzo beans or ceci beans) are served many ways, being a common ingredient in Italian cookery. We start with them dried, then cook them and serve them fried as part of an antipasto platter, in soups, with simple rustic pastas, or what have you. This recipe is Moroccan in inspiration, and is the closest I could come to finding a successful "olive soup."

> 1½ cups dried chick-peas
> 6 cups chicken stock
> 6 tablespoons unsalted butter, at room temperature
> ½ cup Kalamata olives, pitted and chopped
> 1 large potato, unpeeled, diced
> 1 yellow onion, diced
> Hot-pepper flakes
> ½ teaspoon grated fresh ginger
> ½ teaspoon ground turmeric
> Large pinch of crumbled saffron threads
> 2 cinnamon sticks, broken
> 2 teaspoons salt
> Juice of 1 lemon
> 1 cup chopped fresh Italian parsley

Place the chick-peas in a bowl with water to cover. Cover the bowl and refrigerate overnight. The next day, drain the chick-peas and slip off the skins. Transfer the skinned chick-peas to a saucepan and add the chicken stock. Bring to a boil, reduce the heat to medium-low, and simmer until just tender, about 1 hour.

Meanwhile, place the butter in a bowl and, using a wooden spoon, cream it until it is smooth and light. Mix in the olives, distributing them evenly. Form the butter-olive mixture in a ball, cover in plastic wrap, and refrigerate.

In a food processor, combine the cooked chick-peas with a little of the stock from the pan. Purée until almost smooth.

In a large saucepan, stir together the puréed chick-peas, the remaining stock from the pan, the potato, onion, hot-pepper flakes to taste, ginger, turmeric, saffron, cinnamon, salt, and lemon juice. Bring to a simmer, and simmer, uncovered, over medium-low heat for 1 hour. Add most of the parsley, cover, and simmer over low heat for 1 hour longer. Taste and adjust the seasoning.

Ladle the soup into individual bowls and top each serving with a dollop of the chilled butter-olive mixture. Garnish with the remaining parsley.

Serves 6.

Potato and Olive Oil Soup

Here's another rustic recipe by Anzonini del Puerto, the passionate Spanish gypsy, loved by admirers in Spain and Berkeley, who gave to his friends through his piquant cooking and his flamenco music. This soup, called *papas vuida*, is a perfect example of how Anzonini used olive oil to substitute for meat and meat broth and supply a special richness. It is best served the next day, reheated, and ladled into country-style earthen bowls.

> 6 cups water
> 2 ripe tomatoes, peeled, seeded, and chopped
> ½ red bell pepper, seeded and torn into pieces
> 1 large yellow onion, chopped
> 8 cloves garlic, left whole or coarsely chopped
> 1 cup olive oil
> 3 bay leaves
> 10 black peppercorns
> 3 large potatoes, unpeeled, thickly sliced
> Salt

In a large pot, combine the water, tomatoes, bell pepper, onion, garlic, olive oil, bay leaves, and peppercorns. Bring to a boil, reduce the heat to medium-low, cover, and simmer for 45 minutes.

Add the potatoes and simmer until tender, at least 45 minutes longer. The longer it is cooked, the better it becomes. Season to taste with salt. Remove the bay leaves and discard.

Ladle into bowls and serve.

Serves 8.

HOME REMEDIES

Olive oil, and all parts of the olive tree,
figure importantly in potions for all sorts
of ills. Here are some useful recipes:

Olive oil liberally mixed with powdered
charcoal for mushroom poisoning.
Or mixed with crushed seeds of mimosa
against any poison.

Olive oil mixed with an equal part
lime water for burns.

To every quart of olive oil add two hundred
legs of centipedes, a piece of a snake's skin,
and the sprouts of flowered ruda (a Spanish
herb). Boil it until it is reduced by a third.
Good against paralysis.

Leave water that has been used to marinate
olives seven times (once each year for seven
years), and to which salt and fennel have
been added, in the open sun and rain for
forty days. Cures venereal disease.

In a small bottle mix olive oil, chamomile
flowers, anise, and a few cloves of garlic,
finely chopped. Let it sit nine days.
Shake before rubbing on chest, back,
or the soles of feet for coughs, aches, and
soreness, respectively.

MAIN COURSES

Oven-Poached Fish
with Olive Butter

This method of cooking fish poaches it, since no liquid escapes from the foil in which the fish is tightly wrapped. If you are fortunate enough to have a freshly caught steelhead or trout, allow about thirty-five minutes cooking time for a twelve-ounce fish, and allow one fish for two diners. Small, farm-raised salmon are available in many fish markets, but are a good deal less satisfactory in flavor than a fillet of larger salmon fresh from its natural environment. Two eight-ounce fillets of ocean-caught salmon will take about thirty-five minutes to cook by this method, and will serve four diners.

> **For the olive butter:**
> **¼ pound Kalamata or other vinegar-packed black olives, pitted**
> **4 tablespoons unsalted butter, at room temperature**
> **1 tablespoon chopped fresh sweet basil**
>
> **Whole fish or piece of fish (see note above)**
> **Fine olive oil**
> **Garlic slivers**

To make the olive butter, place the olives in a mortar and crush with a pestle to form a paste. Add the butter and basil and beat with a spoon until well combined. Cover and place in the refrigerator to chill.

Preheat an oven to 300°F. Tear off a piece of aluminum foil about 4 inches longer than the fish or piece of fish you are going to bake. Sprinkle some olive oil over the fish and rub to coat all surfaces. Pierce the flesh of the fish every few inches and insert slivers of garlic into the slits. Wrap the fish in the foil, sealing it as well as you can on the top so that no juices leak out or evaporate. Put the fish in a baking pan.

Bake until fish flakes and is opaque throughout; see introduction for timing. Unwrap the fish and serve hot topped with a dollop of the olive butter.

Serves 2 to 4.

Baccalà with Potatoes and Olives

Baccalà is the dried, salted cod that gave Italian grocery stores the smell I disliked as a child. So it came as a surprise to me as an adult that not only are such fish expensive, but they are worth every penny of the cost. The following stew is very good indeed. You may use any brine- or oil-cured black olive.

> **2 pounds dried salt cod, preferably skinless and boneless**
> **½ cup olive oil**
> **6 cloves garlic, minced**
> **5 large yellow onions, diced**
> **3 red bell peppers, seeded and torn into pieces**
> **8 tomatoes, peeled, seeded, and cut into pieces**
> **2 teaspoons dried oregano**
> **2 teaspoons dried thyme**
> **2 bay leaves, broken in half**
> **Freshly ground black pepper**
> **1 ½ cups dry white wine**
> **6 boiling potatoes, unpeeled, cut into slices ½-inch thick**
> **⅔ cup brine- or oil-cured olives such as Niçoise or Ponentine**
> **½ cup chopped fresh Italian parsley**
> **A cruet of fine olive oil**

Place the cod in a bowl and add water to cover. Cover the bowl and refrigerate for 2 days; change the water three times during this period.

Drain the cod and remove any skin, bones, and dark spots. Tear the flesh into small pieces and place in a bowl. Add the ½ cup oil, cover, and marinate the cod for 2 to 3 hours in the refrigerator.

Pour off 2 tablespoons or more of the olive oil used to marinate the fish into a heavy-bottomed pan. Place over medium-high heat. Remove the cod with a slotted utensil and add to the pan. Sauté, stirring once, for 5 minutes. Add an additional tablespoon of the olive oil, the garlic, onions, bell peppers, tomatoes, oregano, thyme, bay leaves, pepper to taste, and the wine. Stir well, bring to a simmer over medium-low heat, cover, and cook for 1½ hours. Add the sliced potatoes, re-cover, and cook, for 25 minutes longer, or until potatoes test done.

Just before serving, stir in the olives and parsley. Check the seasoning; it should be quite peppery. Transfer to a serving dish. Diners should generously douse their servings with fine olive oil. And caution them about the olive pits.

Serves 8.

Baked Rockfish, Veracruz Style

Huachinango a la veracruzana is perhaps Mexico's most famous seafood dish. Around the Gulf of Mexico it is made with red snapper but it can also be made with any local rockfish or firm-fleshed white fish. Two smaller fish may be used in place of a single large fish. This recipe is from the pages of *The California Seafood Cookbook* by Isaac Cronin, Jay Harlow, and Paul Johnson.

> **1 rockfish, 4 to 5 pounds, dressed, or 1½ to 2 pounds white fish**
>   **fillets**
> **Juice of 1 lemon or lime**
> **Salt**
> **2 tablespoons olive oil, plus extra for oiling the baking dish**
> **1 yellow onion, julienned**
> **1 bell pepper, seeded and cut into long, thin strips**
> **1 tablespoon chopped garlic**

2 tomatoes, peeled, seeded, and chopped
¼ cup Sicilian-style olives, pitted and chopped
1 tablespoon capers
2 pickled jalapeño chili peppers, chopped

Preheat an oven to 450°F. Sprinkle the fish with lemon or lime juice and salt and set aside.

In a skillet over medium-high heat, warm the 2 tablespoons olive oil. Add the onion, bell pepper, garlic, and tomatoes and sauté until just softened, about 5 minutes; do not allow to brown. (If using canned tomatoes, add them after the onion and pepper are soft.) Lower the heat and simmer until most of the liquid has evaporated.

If you are using whole fish, oil a deep baking pan and place the fish in it. Pour the tomato sauce over the fish and scatter the olives, capers, and chilies on top. Cover the pan with a tight-fitting lid or foil. Bake 10 minutes for each inch that the fish is thick, or until the flesh flakes easily from the tail; total cooking time will be about 30 minutes. Serve directly from the baking dish with the accumulated sauce from the pan.

If you are using fillets, cut into 4 serving portions. Place each portion on a square of aluminum foil large enough to enclose it completely. Top each with an equal amount of the sauce, olives, capers, and chilies. Fold the foil to enclose the fish completely and seal the edges tightly. Bake until the thickest part of the fillet is about to lose its translucency, 8 to 10 minutes. Open a packet to check for doneness. Serve the packets on individual plates. Let guests unwrap their own.

Serves 4.

Barbecued Pork in Olive Oil Marinade

Here is my attempt to reproduce an unforgettable marinated pork I had in Tepic in western Mexico. Allow the meat at least twelve hours to absorb all the flavors. The pork should be sliced very thin, with the grain, and cooked until just done over good-quality charcoal.

1 pork loin, with or without the bone, 3 to 4 pounds
1 cup olive oil
½ cup white wine vinegar
Tabasco sauce
Sugar
Cumin seeds, finely crushed in a mortar
Salt
Garlic cloves, crushed
1 large yellow onion, thinly sliced into rings and rings separated
Juniper berries
1 bunch fresh cilantro, chopped

Cut the pork with the grain into thin slices. In a high-sided bowl, form a single layer of meat. Sprinkle it with a little of the olive oil, a little of the vinegar, a few dashes of Tabasco sauce, a sprinkling of sugar, a sprinkling of crushed cumin seeds, a sprinkling of salt, a crushed garlic clove, some onion rings, and a few juniper berries, crushing them between your fingers as you add them. Repeat the layers until all the meat is in the bowl, then cover with the remaining olive oil and vinegar. Cover the bowl and marinate in the refrigerator for at least 12 hours or for up to a full day. Remove the meat from the refrigerator a couple hours before grilling to allow it to come to room temperature.

Preheat an oven to 250°F. Light a charcoal fire in a grill. When the coals are medium hot, remove the pork slices from the marinade and arrange the slices on the grill rack along with some of the onion slices. Grill the meat and onions, turning once, until done, about 3 minutes on each side. Remove to a dish and place in the warm oven while the next batch grills. Arrange the pork and onions on a platter, garnish with the cilantro, and serve.

Serves 8.

Moroccan Lamb Tagine
with Prunes and Olives

This typical Moroccan *tagine*, or stew, is easy to make and can be prepared any time of the year. (Tart apples from New Zealand are filling the northern hemisphere late winter and spring apple void.) The sweetness of the prunes and honey is a nice contrast to the bitter olives. Serve the *tagine* over bulgur or couscous.

> 3 tablespoons olive oil
> 3 pounds lamb shoulder, trimmed of fat and cut into
>   bite-size pieces
> 1 teaspoon salt
> Pinch of saffron threads, crushed
> Good pinch of cayenne pepper
> 1 heaping teaspoon finely chopped fresh ginger
> 1/2 teaspoon ground cinnamon
> 1 yellow onion, half minced and half thinly sliced
> 2 cloves garlic, peeled and chopped
> 3/4 cup large brine-cured black olives such as Moroccan or
>   Amfissa
> 1/2 pound prunes, pitted and plumped in warm water
> 1 tablespoon sesame seeds, lightly toasted
> 1 1/2 teaspoons honey
> 1 bunch fresh cilantro, chopped
> 2 tablespoons unsalted butter
> 2 tart apples, peeled, cored, and sliced

In a dutch oven over medium-high heat, warm the olive oil. Add the lamb and sauté, using tongs to turn the lamb pieces to brown on all surfaces. Add the salt, saffron, cayenne, ginger, cinnamon, minced onion, garlic, and water to cover. Stir well, bring to a simmer, cover, and cook over medium-low heat until tender, about 1 hour.

Add the olives, prunes, sesame seeds, honey, cilantro, and sliced onion and stir well. Re-cover and continue to simmer for 5 minutes to blend the flavors.

Meanwhile, in a skillet over medium heat, melt the butter. Add the apple slices and sauté, turning once, until soft, about 10 minutes' total cooking time.

Transfer the *tagine* to a serving dish and garnish with the apple slices. Serve immediately.

Serves 8.

Olive-Stuffed Leg of Lamb

There's nothing like a leg of lamb for a handsome presentation at a special dinner. This Provençal recipe lends itself beautifully to a meat that is not overpowered by a flavorful marinade and stuffing. Serve the lamb on a bed of greens, such as watercress, and surround it with Oven-Fried Potatoes (see page 156). If you have mastered barbecuing lamb, prepare this dish over hot coals; it will taste even better.

2 tablespoons plus 1 cup olive oil
10 cloves garlic
⅓ pound cracked green olives, pitted
2 ounces oil-packed sun-dried tomatoes, drained
1 leg of lamb, 5 to 6 pounds, boned
1 fifth dry white wine
3 bay leaves, broken in half
1 yellow onion, sliced
Salt
Freshly ground black pepper

In a skillet over medium-high heat, warm the 2 tablespoons olive oil. Add the garlic cloves and sauté until golden brown, about 5 minutes. Remove from the heat and place in a bowl.

Chop the olives and tomatoes together finely. Add to the garlic cloves and stir to mix well.

Stuff the lamb with the olive mixture tucking the mixture into the cavity. Tie leg with string, and place it in a high-sided bowl. Pour 1 cup olive oil and all but ½ cup of the wine over the lamb. Add the bay leaves and onion and distribute evenly. Cover the bowl and marinate the lamb in the refrigerator overnight, turning it once before bed and once in the morning.

Remove the meat from the refrigerator a few hours before cooking. Preheat the oven to 400°F.

Place the meat in a roasting pan and put it in the oven. Roast for 15 minutes on the first side; turn and roast 15 minutes longer. Turn down the oven to 350°F and continue roasting until the meat is cooked rare, about 50 minutes longer. The lamb should cook a total of 1 hour and 20 minutes. For medium lamb, add 5 minutes per pound.

Remove the lamb from the oven and transfer to a warmed platter. Tent it with aluminum foil to keep it warm. Place the roasting pan on the stove top. Skim off most of the fat from the pan juices. Bring the juices to a simmer over medium-high heat, add the remaining ½ cup wine, and deglaze the pan by scraping up any browned bits. Reduce the pan juices a little, then season to taste with salt and pepper.

Slice the lamb with the grain, and arrange on the platter. Garnish with the stuffing. Serve the pan juices spooned over the lamb or in a bowl alongside.

Serves 10.

Lamb and Olive Balls

Serve these piquant meatballs on a bed of bulgur with yogurt sauce for a condiment, halved in sandwiches with fruit mustard and greens, or in a spicy tomato sauce over pasta.

3 slices country-style white or whole-wheat bread
2 pounds fairly lean ground lamb
¼ pound feta cheese, crumbled
1 cup Kalamata olives, pitted and chopped
1 egg, beaten
1½ teaspoons ground cinnamon
½ teaspoon hot-pepper flakes
3 cloves garlic, minced
1 bunch fresh cilantro, chopped
3 tablespoons olive oil

Cut the crusts from the bread and discard. Place the slices in a bowl with water to cover barely and let soak for 1 minute. Drain the bread, wring out the slices, and crumble them into a mixing bowl.

Add the lamb, feta, olives, egg, cinnamon, hot-pepper flakes, garlic, and cilantro to the bread crumbs. Using your fingers, mix together until the ingredients are evenly distributed. Form into 10 to 12 large meatballs.

In a heavy frying pan over medium-high heat, warm the olive oil. Add the meatballs and cook until crisp and brown on one side. Then turn the balls until browned on all sides. The cooking time should be no more than about 10 minutes total. The meat should be rare. Serve hot.

Makes 10 to 12 meatballs; serves 5 or 6.

Lamb Shanks with Feta, Red Bell Peppers, and Olives

"This is what beef Stroganoff would have been if it were made by a Greek," said my friend after polishing off a helping. He had failed to see its subtlety: The sweetness of the red bell peppers provides a nice contrast to the saltiness of the feta and olives; the watercress adds a crisp lightness to an otherwise rich dish.

Purists will want to scorch and remove the skins from the peppers before sautéing them (see page 180). The creamier the feta cheese, the smoother the sauce. Bulgur or barley would make a nice accompaniment to this dish.

½ cup olive oil
3 or 4 meaty lamb shanks, cut in half crosswise by the butcher
12 large cloves garlic, 6 unpeeled and 6 peeled
1 tablespoon dried oregano
Salt
Freshly ground black pepper
About ½ cup chicken stock, if needed
¼ pound creamy feta cheese
¼ pound cream cheese, preferably without stabilizers, at room
** temperature**
Scant ¼ cup half-and-half
10 red bell peppers, seeded and cut into long, thin strips
¾ cup dry red wine
1 small bunch fresh basil
1 bunch watercress, stemmed
About 24 Kalamata olives

In a large, heavy skillet over medium-high heat, warm ¼ cup of the olive oil. Add the lamb shanks and brown on all sides, about 10 minutes. Add the 6 unpeeled garlic cloves, the oregano, and salt and pepper to taste. Cover and cook over very low heat until the meat can be easily cut from the bones, about 2 hours. Check periodically to see that the lamb is not scorching. Add the chicken stock to the skillet if it shows signs of scorching.

Meanwhile, put the feta through a food mill, or blend in a blender or food processor until smooth. In a bowl, cream together the feta, cream cheese, and half-and-half. Allow to stand at room temperature.

About 15 minutes before the lamb is ready, in a skillet over medium heat, warm the remaining ¼ cup olive oil. Crush the 6 peeled garlic cloves and add them to the skillet along with the bell peppers, a little salt, and black pepper to taste. Cook uncovered, stirring from time to time, until the bell peppers are tender, about 10 minutes. Keep warm.

Remove the meat and garlic cloves from the skillet to a plate. Cut the meat from its bones in large chunks; keep warm. Skim off the fat from the pan juices. With the skillet over high heat, pour in the wine, deglaze the pan, scraping up any browned bits, and then reduce to thicken to sauce consistency. When the pan juices have thickened sufficiently, remove from the heat and squeeze the whole garlic cloves from their peels into the pan. Add the basil and stir to mix well.

On each dinner plate, arrange a bed of watercress. Divide the meat equally among the plates, placing it in the center of the watercress. Surround the meat with the sautéed peppers. Off center, add a dollop of feta cheese mixture. Pour the thickened pan juices over all and garnish each plate with a few olives.

Serves 4 to 6.

Daube of Beef

There are probably as many different daubes as there are cooks who make them. The unifying characteristic of daubes, however, is that the meat (or a fowl) is braised in wine for a considerable time. A beef daube can be made with a whole rump, or other cut, or with beef cut into pieces as for a stew. It should not be made from a tender, expensive cut, however, because the flavor benefits from the long, slow cooking that only humbler cuts of meat can withstand.

The following daube uses chuck roast cut into large pieces. The *daubiére*—a casserole dish named for the daube and made of stoneware, earthenware, or tinned copper—has here been replaced by a heavy dutch oven that can be left on the stove top for hours.

> **1 cup dried small white beans**
> **¾ cup all-purpose flour**
> **Salt**
> **4 pounds chuck roast, cut into 1½-inch pieces**
> **9 tablespoons olive oil, or as needed**
> **2 cups dry white wine**
> **4 cloves garlic, minced**
> **1 yellow onion, thinly sliced**
> **1 teaspoon dried thyme**
> **2 bay leaves, broken in half**
> **3 wide strips orange zest**
> **Hot-pepper flakes**
> **½ cup tightly packed chopped fresh Italian parsley**
> **2 large carrots, peeled and sliced**
> **10 cherry tomatoes, halved**
> **2 handfuls fresh mushrooms**
> **3 large potatoes, unpeeled, thinly sliced**
> **1 cup small black French olives such as Niçoise**
> **Grated orange zest**
> **Chopped fresh cilantro**

Rinse the beans and place in a saucepan with water to cover. Bring to a boil, then remove from the heat, cover, and let stand for 1 hour. Drain the beans and return them to the pan. Add water to cover, bring to a boil, reduce the heat to medium, cover, and boil gently until almost tender, about 45 minutes. Drain and set aside.

While the beans are cooking, in a shallow dish mix together the flour and 1 teaspoon salt. Dredge the beef in the flour mixture, coating well. In a large dutch oven over medium-high heat, warm 4 tablespoons of the olive oil. Working in batches, add the beef, being careful not to crowd the pan. Using tongs, turn the beef pieces until they are browned on all sides. Remove the browned pieces to a plate and repeat the procedure, adding more oil as necessary, until all the beef is browned.

Return all the beef to the dutch oven. Add the wine, garlic, onion, thyme, bay leaves, orange zest strips, and hot-pepper flakes to taste. Cover and simmer until the meat is about 30 minutes from being done, about 1½ hours. Taste and adjust the salt. Add the parsley, carrots, tomatoes, and the reserved cooked beans. Cover and simmer until the beef and beans are tender, about 30 minutes longer.

Meanwhile, in a large skillet over medium high heat, warm 3 tablespoons of the olive oil. Add the mushrooms and sauté until they are done, that is, until they no longer absorb oil. This should take about 5 minutes. Remove from the pan and set aside.

Spread the sliced potatoes in the same frying pan and dribble 2 tablespoons olive oil over them. Salt lightly and cover the pan. Cook over low heat until tender, about 20 minutes.

When the beef is done, stir in the mushrooms and olives. Transfer the potatoes to a warmed platter and spoon the beef mixture over the top. Garnish with grated orange zest and cilantro.

Serves 6.

Beef Tongue with Piquant Sauce

I first had this informal dish while staying in Sarlat, in the south of France. The sauce is a delicious pickle, good with any boiled meat—ham, fowl, or, as here, tongue. It tastes best if made a few days in advance of serving and stored tightly capped in the refrigerator. The sauce will keep for up to a week.

1 beef tongue, about 2½ pounds
30 juniper berries, crushed
2 cinnamon sticks
3 bay leaves, broken in half
1½ teaspoons salt

For the piquant sauce:
1 pound pearl onions, peeled
2 tomatoes, peeled and chopped
1 can (6 ounces) tomato paste, or, preferably, ¾ cup homemade tomato paste (see page 181)
7 tablespoons cider vinegar
1 cup raisins
½ cup water
1 cup Sicilian-style olives, pitted and chopped
3 tablespoons brown sugar
3 pinches of cayenne pepper
¼ teaspoon ground cinnamon
Dried thyme
1 cup walnut halves, cut in half lengthwise and toasted

Place the tongue in a large saucepan with water to cover by about 2 inches. Add the juniper berries, cinnamon sticks, bay leaves, and salt. Bring to a boil, reduce the heat to medium-low, cover, and simmer until tender, about 2½ hours.

Remove the tongue from the pan and allow to cool to room temperature.

While the tongue is cooking, prepare the sauce. Fill a saucepan three-fourths full with water and bring to a boil. Add the onions and boil for

10 minutes. Drain well and return to the saucepan. Add the tomatoes, tomato paste, vinegar, raisins, water, olives, sugar, cayenne, cinnamon, and thyme to taste. Stir well and bring to a simmer over medium heat. Cover and continue to simmer over medium-low heat until the raisins are plump, about 5 minutes. Stir in the walnuts and remove from the heat. Let cool to room temperature.

Skin the tongue and trim away any gristle, fat, and bones. Slice and arrange on a platter. Serve at room temperature with the sauce on the side.

Serves 6.

Carne Rellenada

A succulent Spanish beef dish that can be served cool (after being weighted in a deep dish in the refrigerator), or hot with its wonderful gravy. This is one of the most aromatic dishes I know, and one of the prettiest when sliced, with the yellow eggs and red peppers forming a spiral.

> **Olive oil**
> **3 eggs, beaten**
> **2 red bell peppers, seeded and cut into long, thin strips**
> **3 carrots, peeled and cut into thin strips**
> **1 flank steak, about 2 pounds, butterflied**
> **3 cloves garlic, crushed**
> **Salt**
> **Freshly ground black pepper**
> **1/2 pound Spanish- or Italian-style pork sausages**
> **2/3 cup Spanish-style green olives, pitted and chopped**
> **All-purpose flour for dredging**
> **2 cups homemade beef stock or canned chicken broth**
> **1 cup dry white wine**
> **1 yellow onion, quartered**
> **1 tomato, quartered**
> **2 bay leaves, crumbled**

In an omelet pan or skillet over medium-high heat, warm a little olive oil. Add the eggs and tilt the pan to cover the bottom evenly. Cook, lifting edges to allow uncooked egg to flow underneath, until firmly set, about 3 minutes. Slide the omelet out of the pan onto a cutting surface and cut into 1/2-inch-wide strips; set aside.

In a skillet over medium heat, warm 1/4 cup olive oil. Add the bell peppers and carrots and sauté until barely tender, about 15 minutes. Set aside.

Rub the butterflied steak with the garlic, then sprinkle it with salt and pepper. Remove the raw sausages from their casings and crumble them over the steak.

Arrange the bell peppers and carrots and the omelet strips over the steak, laying them lengthwise with the grain. Finally, sprinkle the olives evenly over the steak. Starting at one long end, roll up the steak and tie securely with string in several places.

Dredge the stuffed steak in flour. In a dutch oven or other heavy pot over medium-high heat, warm ¼ cup olive oil. Add the beef roll and brown on all sides, about 15 minutes. Add the stock, wine, onion, tomato, and bay leaves. Cover and simmer over low heat until the roll is tender, 1 to 1½ hours.

If the meat is to be served hot, transfer it to a cutting board. Clip and remove the strings, then slice the beef roll and arrange on a warmed platter. Strain the gravy into a sauceboat.

If the meat is to be served cold, put the rolled steak into a pan in which it fits snugly. Clip and remove the strings, then strain the gravy over the meat. Top the meat with a heavy plate topped with a weight and refrigerate for at least 2 hours before slicing. Discard the gravy.

Serves 8.

Moroccan Chicken with Cracked Green Olives

Served whole and tinted with saffron, this chicken makes a handsome presentation. Carve the chicken at the table and serve with plenty of the lemony gravy.

>2 cups (about ¾ pound) cracked green olives
>4 tablespoons olive oil
>1 chicken, 3½ to 4 pounds
>Salt
>Freshly ground black pepper
>1 teaspoon fresh ginger, minced
>3 cloves garlic, minced
>1 tablespoon cumin seeds, finely ground in a mortar or spice
> grinder
>Large pinch of saffron threads, crushed
>2½ cups chicken stock, preferably homemade
>Red-leaf lettuce leaves or curly endive
>¼ cup fresh lemon juice
>Grated zest of 1 lemon

Pit the olives, then place in a saucepan with water to cover. Bring to a boil and boil for 15 minutes. Drain and repeat with fresh water, then drain again. (This boiling process makes the olives less bitter, but dulls their bright green color.) Set aside.

In a large dutch oven over medium-high heat, warm 2 tablespoons of the olive oil. Add the whole chicken and brown well on all sides, about 15 minutes. Remove from the pan to a plate and sprinkle with salt and pepper. Set aside.

Drain off the fat from the pan. Warm the remaining 2 tablespoons oil in the same pan over medium heat. Add the ginger, garlic, cumin, and saffron and sauté for 1 minute. Then add the chicken stock and stir well.

Return the chicken to the pot, cover, and cook for 12 minutes on one side. Turn the chicken over, re-cover, and cook for 12 minutes on the other side.

The chicken should be just done; test by piercing with a knife tip. If it is not ready, cook for a few more minutes, and test again.

Arrange a bed of lettuce on a serving platter. Remove the chicken from the liquid and place it on the lettuce. Add the lemon juice to the liquid in the pot and reduce over high heat until the sauce is slightly thickened. Add the olives and heat just long enough to warm them through. Using a slotted spoon, distribute the olives over the chicken.

Pour the sauce into a bowl and serve alongside the chicken. Garnish the chicken with the lemon zest.

Serves 4.

Chicken with Feta and Kalamata Olives

This savory Greek-inspired dish was adapted from a recipe by Ann Walker, a Bay Area caterer known for her robust cuisine.

$\frac{1}{2}$ **cup all-purpose flour**
1 teaspoon salt
$\frac{1}{2}$ **teaspoon freshly ground black pepper**
$\frac{1}{2}$ **teaspoon dried marjoram**
$\frac{1}{2}$ **teaspoon dried oregano**
1 frying chicken, about 3 pounds, cut into serving pieces
$\frac{1}{4}$ **cup olive oil**
1 cup chicken stock, preferably homemade
Juice of 1 lemon
2 cups fresh or canned peeled tomatoes, chopped, with their juice
25 Kalamata olives
1 large clove garlic, crushed
$\frac{1}{2}$ **pound feta, crumbled**
2 tablespoons fresh green or red basil or other fresh
  Mediterranean herb such as oregano or thyme

Stir together the flour, salt, pepper, and dried marjoram, or oregano in a shallow dish. Dredge the chicken in the flour mixture; reserve the remaining flour mixture.

In a large skillet over medium-high heat, warm the olive oil until a haze forms above it. Add the chicken pieces and brown on all sides, about 10 minutes. (Cook the legs and thighs a little longer than the breasts and wings.) Remove the chicken to a heavy, lidded dutch oven.

Drain off all but 2 tablespoons of the fat from the skillet. Place the skillet over low heat and stir in 3 tablespoons of the reserved flour mixture. Gradually add the stock and lemon juice, stirring with a wire whisk until thick and smooth.

Add the tomatoes and their juice, olives, and garlic and stir well. Pour over the chicken. Cover and cook over medium heat until the chicken breasts are just tender when pierced, about 30 minutes.

Scatter the feta on top, cover, and cook for a few minutes longer until the cheese melts. Transfer to a serving dish and garnish with the fresh herb. Serve immediately.

Serves 4.

Chicken with Leeks, Tarragon, Orange, and Olives

Fresh tarragon is critical to the success of this delicate, refreshing dish, as the character of dried tarragon is quite different. Serve with polenta (see page 98) or potatoes mashed with roasted garlic.

> **⅓ cup all-purpose flour**
> **Salt**
> **Freshly ground black pepper**
> **1 frying chicken, about 3½ pounds, cut into serving pieces**
> **3 leeks**
> **¼ cup olive oil**
> **4 cups chicken stock, preferably homemade**
> **1 orange, peeled and very thinly sliced**
> **2 teaspoons chopped fresh tarragon**
> **1 cup small, brine-cured black olives such as Elitses or Ponentine**

In a paper bag, combine the flour, 1 teaspoon salt, and pepper to taste. Add chicken parts, and shake well to coat.

Halve the leeks lengthwise, wash thoroughly, then halve crosswise. In a large dutch oven over high heat, warm the olive oil until very hot. Place the leeks, side by side and cut sides down, in the oil. Cook until browned. Remove from the pan and set aside. Add the chicken pieces to the pan and brown on all sides, about 10 minutes, cooking the legs and thighs a little longer than the breasts and wings. Remove to paper towels to drain.

Drain off the fat from the pan and return the chicken and leeks to it. Pour in the chicken stock and distribute the orange slices and tarragon evenly among the chicken pieces. Cover and simmer over medium heat until the breasts are just tender when pierced, about 30 minutes.

Meanwhile, preheat the oven to 250°F. When the chicken is ready, remove it to a warmed platter and place in the oven. Bring the liquid and the leeks to a boil and cook uncovered until the leeks are tender, just a few minutes. Using a slotted spoon, remove the leeks and arrange them attractively around the chicken. Return the platter to the oven.

Now cook the liquid at a rapid boil until it is reduced and thickened. Add the olives, taste, adjust the salt, and pour the sauce over the chicken. Serve immediately.

Serves 4.

Rabbit Stew with Olives

Rabbit has never become popular in America, despite the fine qualities of the succulent, juicy meat. If good fresh rabbit is available to you, the following recipe makes a tasty, hearty stew. Most commercial rabbits weigh 2½ to 3 pounds, so you will need two of them to make this dish. Larger, older rabbits may take longer to cook.

Serve the stew over fresh *pappardelle*. Cut into ribbons about ¾-inch wide or wider. Pass a robust bread for sopping up the thick, plentiful gravy this recipe makes.

>   ¾ **cup all-purpose flour**
>   **Freshly ground black pepper**
>   **Salt**
>   **6 pounds rabbit, cut into serving pieces (see introduction)**
>   ⅓ **cup olive oil, or as needed**
>   **3 cups chicken stock**
>   **2 cups dry white wine**
>   **1 large head garlic, cloves peeled and left whole**
>   **3 bay leaves, broken in half**
>   **1 cup finely chopped fresh Italian parsley**
>   **1 teaspoon dried thyme**
>   ¼ **cup commercial or, preferably, homemade tomato paste**
>   **(see page 181)**
>   ¼ **pound hot coppa or ham, cut into long, thin strips**
>   ½ **pound dry-cured black olives**
>   **Grated zest of 1 lemon**

Stir together the flour, a good dose of finely ground pepper, and about 1 teaspoon salt in a shallow dish. Dredge the rabbit pieces in the flour mixture. In a large dutch oven over medium-high heat, warm ⅓ cup olive oil. Add the rabbit pieces and brown well on all sides, about 15 minutes, removing them to drain on paper towels as they are done and adding more olive oil if necessary. When all the pieces are browned, pour off the fat and wipe the pan clean.

Return the meat to the pan and add the chicken stock, wine, garlic, bay leaves, ½ cup of the parsley, thyme, and tomato paste. Stir well, bring to simmer over medium-high heat, reduce the heat to medium-low, and cook until the rabbit is tender, up to 1¾ hours, depending on the age of the animal. Add the coppa and olives and cook for 5 minutes longer. Taste and adjust the seasonings.

Transfer to a serving dish and garnish with the remaining ½ cup parsley and the lemon zest. Serve hot.

Serves 8.

Duck with Wine and Olives

The following recipe provides a number of flavors and textures that balance each other beautifully: the richness of the duck meat is cut by the tart lemon zest and complemented by the sweet wine; the soft cooked onions and firm olives are enveloped by fragrant garlic and thyme, the flavors of Provence.

> **1 duck, 4 to 5 pounds, with giblets and neck**
> **Salt**
> **2 yellow onions**
> **1¼ cups sweet, fruity wine such as a Spätlese or Muscat**
> **1 teaspoon dried thyme**
> **6 small cloves garlic**
> **A few strips lemon zest**
> **Freshly ground black pepper**
> **¼ pound small olives such as Niçoise, Picholine, or Ponentine**
> **Watercress**

Preheat an oven to 425°F. Remove the wing tips from the bird, as they will burn upon roasting; set them aside. Remove the excess fat from the neck end of the bird and from the body cavity. Rub the bird inside and out with salt. Cut up 1 of the onions and put the pieces in the body cavity. Truss the duck as you would a chicken to keep the wings and legs close to the body. With a fork, poke the bird all over at close intervals so the fat can escape as the bird cooks.

Put the duck, breast side up, in a roasting pan. Roast until lightly browned, about 20 minutes. Turn the bird over; reduce the heat to 350°F and roast for 1½ hours longer. (If you prefer pink meat, cook the duck a total of 1¼ hours or until the juices run a pale pink when the bird is pricked near the thigh joint. The less-done bird has better flavor and moisture, but can be a little tougher.)

While the duck roasts, make a stock. In a saucepan combine the gizzard, neck, heart, and wing tips and add water to cover. Coarsely chop the remaining onion and add to the pan. Bring to a boil, reduce the heat to medium, cover, and simmer for an hour or so. Strain the stock and return the liquid to the pan. Place over high heat and reduce to ¼ cup.

When the duck is ready, remove it to a warmed plate and tent with aluminum foil to keep warm. Using a bulb baster, remove the roasting pan juices from beneath the fat and add to the reduced stock. Add the wine, thyme, garlic, lemon zest, a pinch of salt, and pepper to taste. Place the pan over high heat and reduce the liquid by half. Add the olives and heat through.

Arrange the watercress in a bed on a platter. Cut the duck into serving pieces and place on the watercress. Pour the sauce over all and serve.

Serves 3 or 4.

SALADS AND
VEGETABLES

Country-Style Greek Salad

Vary this salad according to what is in season and your tastes and preferences. Many believe it must include spinach, and, indeed, spinach goes very well with the feta cheese. Be sure not to overpower the salad with any one herb or full-flavored green, and don't confuse the dish with too many aromatic flavors. A purple onion, sliced paper-thin, is wonderful with the anchovies and feta. A good rule of thumb for feta cheese is to allow two ounces per person. Be careful lest you put too much vinegar in the dressing, or too much dressing on the salad. Serve the salad with a hearty country-style bread and unsalted butter.

Lettuces such as frisée, red leaf, and curly endive
Spinach leaves, stemmed
Thinly sliced purple onion
Arugula
Watercress
A fresh herb such as mint, cilantro, basil, or thyme
Peeled, seeded, and thinly sliced cucumber
Greek brine-cured black olives
Crumbled feta cheese
Capers
Minced garlic cloves
Salt
Freshly ground black pepper
Anchovy fillets, rinsed and chopped
Greek fine olive oil
Red wine vinegar

In a large bowl, combine all the ingredients for the salad except olive oil and vinegar. Drizzle with the olive oil and vinegar to taste and toss well. Serve at once.

Greek Fish Salad with Avgolemono Sauce

This cool, delicate salad makes a refreshing hot-day lunch or an elegant first course. Use halibut, swordfish, or other firm-fleshed fish.

3 tablespoons olive oil
2 cups water
2 bay leaves, broken in half
6 black peppercorns
1 small yellow onion, sliced
1 small lemon, sliced
2 pounds thick fish fillets or steaks (see introduction)

For the avgolemono sauce:
2 egg yolks
½ cup fish stock, from cooking fish, heated
1½ tablespoons fresh lemon juice
½ cup créme fraîche
½ teaspoon salt

1 cucumber, peeled, seeded, and sliced
12 cherry tomatoes, halved
24 Greek olives, either Kalamata or Amphissa

In a skillet over medium-low heat, combine the olive oil, water, bay leaves, peppercorns, onion, and lemon. Cover and simmer for 5 minutes. Add the fish pieces, side by side, cover, and cook until done, 5 to 8 minutes, depending on the thickness of the fish. Check for doneness with a fork after 5 minutes and remove from the heat just before cooked. The fish will continue to cook for about 1 minute after it has been removed from the heat. Carefully remove the fish from the liquid and place on a plate. Let cool to room temperature. (Or let cool, cover, and refrigerate, then bring to room temperature before serving.) Over high heat, reduce the liquid in the pan to ½ cup and use for making the sauce.

To prepare the sauce, in the top of a double boiler or bain-marie placed over simmering water, whisk the egg yolks with a wire whisk and slowly add the hot fish stock. Add the lemon juice and cook, whisking constantly, until the sauce thickens. Remove from the heat, mix in the crème fraîche, and season with salt to taste. Let cool, cover, and refrigerate.

To assemble the salad, divide the fish into 8 serving pieces and divide the pieces among 8 serving plates. Arrange the cucumber slices and tomato halves around the fish pieces. Pour the chilled sauce over all. Garnish with the olives.

Serves 8.

Belgian Endive Salad

Soak 3 Belgian endives in ice water for 30 minutes. Shake the water out. Cut them crosswise into very thin slices and place in a salad bowl. Toss with 2 tablespoons fine olive oil; about 10 Kalamata or other vinegar-packed olives, pitted and finely chopped; 1 teaspoon sherry vinegar; 2 anchovy fillets, rinsed and finely chopped; and salt and freshly ground black pepper to taste.

Serves 3.

Salade Niçoise

There are no strict recipes for this famous salad, for the ingredients depend on what vegetables are in season. Choose a few from each category below. Certain ingredients are a must: first-rate olive oil, red wine vinegar, garlic, and olives, preferably Niçoise or Niçoise-type (small, black, and brine-cured). Tuna, of course, is also is a necessary ingredient in this wonderful composed salad.

Red wine vinegar
A soft, fine olive oil
Minced garlic

Lettuces and other greens:
  Bibb
  Red leaf
  Curly endive
  Frisée
  Romaine
  Spinach
  Watercress
  Arugula
  Radicchio

Raw vegetables:
  Summer squashes
  Radishes
  Green onions
  Tender green peas
  Fennel bulbs
  Tomatoes

Parboiled vegetables:
  Asparagus
  Broccoli
  Carrots
  Cauliflower
  Green beans
  Bell peppers

Boiled or steamed foods:
  Potatoes
  Hard-cooked eggs (see page 179)
  Artichoke hearts
  Tuna fillet

Additional flavors:
  Kosher salt
  Freshly ground black pepper
  Niçoise olives
  Anchovy fillets, rinsed
  Capers

Arrange your *salade niçoise* as artfully as possible, on a large, pretty platter. Start with a selection of lettuces and other leafy greens in a bowl. Dress them with a mixture of vinegar, oil, and garlic and toss well. Arrange them on the serving platter. Next, slice the raw vegetables as appropriate (thin, whenever possible), fan them, and arrange atop the greens to one side. Arrange the parboiled vegetables, sliced, when appropriate, and fanned, on the opposite side, leaving the center of the salad open. Arrange the potatoes in a small mound, and slice and fan the hard-cooked eggs. Place the tuna in the center and, using a fork, break it apart into large chunks.

Dress all but the greens with a vinaigrette made with minced garlic, red wine vinegar, and the best olive oil you have. Sprinkle with Kosher salt and pepper to taste. Garnish with olives, anchovies, and capers.

Onion, Olive, and Lettuce Salad

Serve this simple and refreshing salad on a hot summer afternoon or evening. The onions, which "cook" a little in the dressing, are tame enough not to overpower the rest of the meal.

1 large purple onion, sliced paper-thin
¼ cup fine olive oil
3 tablespoons rice vinegar
¼ teaspoon salt
Freshly ground black pepper
1 cup Elitses or Kalamata olives
1 bunch watercress, stemmed
A mixture of lettuces such as frisée, red leaf, escarole, and so on, equaling 1 bunch
½ bunch or head bitter greens such as arugula or radicchio

Place the onion in a bowl. Pour the olive oil and vinegar over the top. Add the salt and season to taste with pepper. Let stand for a few hours at room temperature, tossing from time to time. Add the olives and toss again.

Tear the lettuces and bitter greens into bite-size pieces and place in a salad bowl. Add the olives and onions with their marinade. Toss well and serve.

Serves 6.

Pasta and Olive Salad

Many varieties of pasta are available now, and their beautiful shapes make handsome salads. Most chefs prefer *fusilli* or similar pastas for salads; there is more surface area for the dressing to coat than with the larger flat types, an important factor with pasta salads.

This dish travels well on picnics since it contains no immediately perishable ingredients. Or it can be placed on a buffet table with cold cuts and other salads. If you like, cold poached salmon or tuna or leftover rare grilled beef can be added to the salad; correct the seasonings as needed.

> **1 pound dried pasta, either rice-shaped (*rosamarina* or *semini di melo*) or intricately shaped (*fusilli* or *farfalle*)**
> **3 tablespoons fine olive oil**
> **1 large clove garlic, minced**
> **1 tablespoon balsamic vinegar**
> **1/3 cup Sicilian-style (green) olives, pitted and finely chopped**
> **1/4 cup finely chopped roasted red bell pepper (see page 180)**
> **2 green onions, cut into threadlike pieces about 1 inch long**
> **1/4 cup finely chopped fresh Italian parsley**
> **Pinch of fresh thyme, oregano, or marjoram**
> **Salt**
> **Freshly ground black pepper**

Bring a large pot filled with salted water to a rapid boil. Plunge the pasta into the water. Stir and cook until al dente; timing will depend on shape and brand of pasta. Pour into a colander and let drain for a few minutes, then transfer to a large bowl.

Add the olive oil to the pasta and toss well while hot. Add the garlic, vinegar, olives, bell pepper, green onions, parsley, and herb. Toss again to mix well; season to taste with salt and pepper and let cool. Serve at room temperature.

Serves 4 to 6.

Parsley and Olive Salad

Although this rich salad is a fine accompaniment for Italian cured meats such as *coppa* and *soppressata* and good Tuscan or sourdough bread, it can also serve as a condiment to grilled chops or roast fowl.

> **1 cup firmly packed, pitted and chopped Sicilian-style green olives**
> **¼ cup chopped roasted red bell pepper (see page 180)**
> **1 cup walnuts, toasted and chopped**
> **2 cups coarsely chopped fresh Italian parsley**
> **3½ tablespoons fine olive oil**
> **1 tablespoon fresh lemon juice**
> **1½ teaspoons capers, chopped**
> **1 large clove garlic, minced**
> **Hot-pepper flakes**

Combine the olives, bell pepper, walnuts, parsley, olive oil, lemon juice, capers, and garlic in a salad bowl. Season with hot-pepper flakes to taste. Toss to mix thoroughly. Serve at room temperature.

Serves 6.

Tuna, Rice, and Olive Salad

Offer this rich salad on a buffet with cold meats, a variety of other salads, breads, and cheeses. Serve at room temperature, but be sure to refrigerate it if you are preparing it ahead of time. It will remain safe at room temperature for at least an hour. Aioli is perishable.

4 cups water
Salt
2 cups Arborio rice
1½ recipes Aioli (see page 84)
1½ cups Sicilian-style green olives, pitted and coarsely chopped
2 celery hearts, diced
½ pound tuna fillet, poached and broken into large pieces
Freshly ground black pepper
2 ripe tomatoes, sliced
2 hard-cooked eggs (see page 179), cut into wedges
8 anchovy fillets, rinsed
½ bunch fresh Italian parsley, chopped

Pour the water into a saucepan and bring to a boil. Add salt to taste, pour in the rice, and stir well. Reduce the heat to low, cover, and simmer until the rice is tender but still chewy, about 35 minutes. Check near the end of cooking and add a little more water if the rice has dried out before it is cooked. Pour the rice into a sieve, rinse with cold water, and let drain.

In a bowl thoroughly combine the drained rice, ¼ teaspoon salt, the Aioli, olives, celery hearts, tuna, and pepper to taste. Taste and adjust the seasonings. Transfer to a serving dish and garnish with the tomatoes, eggs, and anchovy fillets. Sprinkle with the parsley and serve.

Serves 8.

Armenian Eggplant Salad

This salad is best freshly made and cooled to room temperature.

1 eggplant, about 1 pound
Salt
Olive oil
1 small purple onion, finely chopped
½ bunch fresh Italian parsley, finely chopped
1 tablespoon rice vinegar
½ teaspoon ground cinnamon
Freshly ground black pepper

Cut the unpeeled eggplant into 1-inch chunks. Put the chunks in a large bowl, then sprinkle them with salt and shake the bowl well. Place a weight such as a heavy plate atop the eggplant and let stand for 1 hour or so. Drain off any liquid in the bottom of the bowl.

In a heavy skillet over medium heat, pour in olive oil to a depth of ¼ inch. When the oil is hot, add the eggplant and leave the pieces unturned until they are browned a bit; then turn and cook until the chunks are lightly browned on all sides, about 15 minutes total cooking time. Add oil as necessary to keep the eggplant from sticking. The eggplant will be done when it no longer absorbs oil.

Transfer the eggplant to a serving dish. Add the onion, parsley, vinegar, cinnamon, and pepper and toss well. Let cool to room temperature and serve.

Serves 6.

Pear, Watercress, and Olive Salad

Juicy, sweet pears and a peppery olive oil are equally balanced in this salad, which is especially good following a heavy main course.

1 large or 2 smaller ripe pears, peeled and cored
Juice of ½ Meyer or other lemon
2 tablespoons mild fine olive oil such as Provençal
¼ cup Elitses, Niçoise, or Ligurian olives
Pinch of salt
1 bunch watercress, stemmed

Cut the pear(s) into ½-inch cubes. Place in a bowl. Add the lemon juice, olive oil, olives, and salt and toss well.

Line 4 salad plates with the watercress. Divide the pear mixture evenly among the plates and pour any dressing remaining in the bottom of the bowl over the watercress. Serve at once.

Serves 4.

White Beans, Oliveto Style

We serve beans with any number of rustic meals at Oliveto Restaurant, and even as one of our *contorni* for those who love them. Puréed and flavored with rosemary, they make a perfect topping for *crostini*. Although not difficult to cook, there are a few rules to follow to make them perfect.

The only beans we serve at Oliveto that have to be soaked overnight are chick-peas (garbanzos or ceci beans) and cannellini beans. They will triple in size during this time. For all the others, we simply bring them to a boil in water (never cook them in salted water–they have a tendency to break apart when salted). Remove from heat and let them sit, covered, for 1 hour. A good ratio is 1 cup beans to 3 or 4 cups water. Drain.

In a large, heavy casserole over medium heat, fry a scrap of *pancetta* or prosciutto in ¼ cup olive oil until its flavor is released. Add a halved onion, cut sides down; 1 large carrot, cut into quarters; and 2 stalks celery, cut in half. Cook over medium-high heat until the onion and carrots are caramelized, about 15 minutes. Add the beans, a few bay leaves, and a sprig of fresh thyme to the pot and stir until completely coated with the olive oil and vegetable juices.

Add chicken stock to cover by 1 or 2 inches. Bring to a simmer (do not boil); do not add salt. Cover and simmer until tender, about 1 hour.

Beans thus cooked do very well reheated after refrigeration. Simply reheat in the liquid in which they were cooked. Remove and discard the bay leaves. Season to taste with salt and pepper before serving, or purée and gratinée for the dish of your choice.

Makes 3 cups.

Squash Gratin with Garlic and Olive Oil

A gratin is any dish cooked in such a way that it forms a nice crust on top. The crust is most commonly accomplished by topping the dish with bread crumbs or grated aged cheese and putting the dish under a broiler. A gratin can also be prepared as in this recipe, by long baking uncovered in the oven.

About 3 pounds butternut or other firm winter squash
8 cloves garlic, finely minced
1 large bunch fresh Italian parsley, finely chopped
5 tablespoons all-purpose flour
Salt
Freshly ground black pepper
⅔ cup olive oil
½ cup toasted fine dried bread crumbs (page 177)

Preheat an oven to 350°F.

Peel and seed the squash. Cut it into ⅓-inch cubes. In a large bowl, toss the squash with the garlic and parsley. Then sprinkle in the flour and salt and pepper to taste and toss until all the cubes are coated with the flour.

Oil a large gratin dish or a wide, shallow baking dish with a little of the olive oil. Spread the squash in the dish. Sprinkle the bread crumbs over the top. Dribble the remaining olive oil over the squash in a crisscross fashion. Bake until the top of the squash has formed a crisp, brown crust, about 2 hours.

Serve hot from the oven.

Serves 8.

Artichokes à la Grecque

If you like, prepare this dish up to a day ahead of time, cover, and refrigerate. Remove it from the refrigerator long enough before serving for the oil to liquefy. It needs the shiny black olives to liven its somewhat drab colors.

8 artichokes
¾ cup fresh lemon juice
Salt
8 small carrots, peeled and cut in half lengthwise
2 potatoes, unpeeled, cut into ½-inch cubes
1 cup olive oil
2 tablespoons chopped fresh dill
2 bunches green onions, trimmed but left whole
Freshly ground black pepper
24 plump dry-cured olives

Trim the tough outer leaves and the stem ends from the artichokes; cut off about ½ inch from the tops. Cut the artichokes in half lengthwise and scoop out and remove the chokes. Rub the cut sides of the artichokes with a little of the lemon juice and then immerse them in a bowl of salted water, to which ¼ cup of the lemon juice has been added to prevent their discoloration.

In a large skillet (not iron) with a lid, or in a dutch oven, place the artichokes, flat sides down, carrots, potatoes, olive oil, dill, salt to taste, the remaining lemon juice, and almost enough water to cover the artichokes. Cover and simmer over medium heat until the artichokes are nearly cooked, about 20 minutes. Add the green onions and cook for 5 minutes longer.

Transfer the artichokes to a serving platter, pouring the sauce from the pan over the top. Sprinkle with pepper. Garnish with the olives and serve at room temperature.

Serves 8.

Savory Fennel

Fennel, with its faint licorice flavor, has such a nice, crisp texture and delicate flavor I wonder why it isn't seen more often as an accompaniment for chops, roasts, and other meats, or as an ingredient in salads. Its only flaw is an aesthetic one: it is a pale, translucent green when cooked, and, when placed on a plate, requires a bit of color to show it off.

> **5 tablespoons olive oil**
> **1 large yellow onion, thinly sliced**
> **1 tablespoon chopped fresh rosemary**
> **2 tablespoons toasted fine dried bread crumbs (see page 177)**
> **Salt**
> **3 large fennel bulbs, trimmed and halved lengthwise**
> **1 cup dry white wine**
> **Freshly ground black pepper**
> **Crushed fennel seeds**

In a large, flat-bottomed skillet over medium heat, warm 2 tablespoons of the olive oil. Add the onion and rosemary and sauté until the onion slices are tender, about 7 minutes. Add the bread crumbs and cook the mixture until it is golden, about 5 minutes. Sprinkle to taste with salt. Transfer to a bowl and set aside. Wipe the pan clean and return it to the stove top.

Add the remaining 3 tablespoons olive oil to the pan and warm it over low heat. Place the fennel bulbs, flat sides down, in the oil, cover, and cook until lightly browned, about 10 minutes. Add the wine and season to taste with salt and pepper. Cover and cook until the fennel is tender, about 20 minutes.

Meanwhile, preheat an oven to 300°F. When the fennel is ready, transfer it to a warmed serving platter, reserving the liquid in the pan. Place the fennel in the warm oven.

Raise the heat to high and boil the liquid in the skillet until it has a thick consistency. Pour over the fennel. Return the onion mixture to the pan and reheat for 1 minute. Top the fennel with the onion mixture. Garnish with the fennel seeds and serve.

Serves 6.

Ratatouille

Although time-consuming, cooking the vegetables separately preserves the individual textures and flavors of this popular and aromatic eggplant stew and is essential to its success. You will need a covered, thick-bottomed four-quart pot, a skillet, and three bowls.

> **1 eggplant, about 1 pound**
> **Salt**
> **3 zucchini, about ⅔ pound total weight, sliced ¼-inch thick**
> **½ cup plus 3 tablespoons olive oil**
> **Freshly ground black pepper**
> **2 yellow onions, thinly sliced**
> **2 red bell peppers, seeded and cut lengthwise into thin strips**
> **4 cloves garlic, minced**
> **4 tomatoes, peeled, seeded, and chopped**
> **½ cup chopped fresh cilantro**

Peel the eggplant, cut into rounds ½ inch thick, and then slice into rectangles 2 inches long by 1 inch wide. Put the eggplant in a bowl, sprinkle with salt, and toss well. Put the zucchini in another bowl, sprinkle with salt and toss well. Let the vegetables stand to sweat for 30 minutes, then pat the eggplant and zucchini pieces dry with a cloth towel.

In a skillet over medium-high heat, warm ¼ cup of the olive oil. Add the eggplant and sauté until lightly browned, about 10 minutes, adding more olive oil if necessary. Season to taste with pepper. Transfer to a bowl and set aside.

In the same skillet, warm another ¼ cup olive oil. Add the zucchini and sauté until lightly browned but not limp, about 5 minutes. Season to taste with pepper; transfer to another bowl and set aside.

In the same skillet over medium-high heat, warm 2 tablespoons of the olive oil. Add the onions, bell peppers, and garlic and sauté until the vegetables are tender, about 5 minutes. Season to taste with salt and pepper; transfer to another bowl, and set aside.

In the same skillet over medium heat, warm the remaining 1 tablespoon olive oil. Add the tomatoes and cook until the liquid they exude evaporates, stirring occasionally. Remove from the heat.

In a 4-quart pot, layer half of the eggplant. Top with half of the zucchini, half of the pepper-onion mixture, half of the cilantro, and half of the tomatoes. Repeat the layers with the remaining ingredients.

Cover and simmer over low heat for 10 minutes. Uncover and, with a bulb baster, baste the stew with juices from the bottom of the dish. Continue to simmer, uncovered, until the juices are absorbed, about 10 minutes more; be careful not to scorch the bottom.

Serve hot as a vegetable side dish, or cold as a salad or antipasto.

Serves 4 to 6.

Oven-Fried Potatoes

Pour 1 cup olive oil into a 12-by-18-inch baking pan. Slice 4 or 5 baking potatoes into ⅓-inch-thick rounds. Rub the slices with olive oil on both sides and place them in the pan. Sprinkle with salt. Bake uncovered for 30 minutes at 400°F; turn with a spatula and bake until crispy brown, another 15 minutes or so. They make a nice accompaniment for roasts or highly seasoned meats.

Serves 6.

Broccoli Sautéed in Olive Oil

Parboil broccoli florets and drain well. Sauté them quickly in plenty of olive oil with minced garlic. Season with salt and freshly ground black pepper to taste. Add finely chopped Kalamata olives at the end if you like. Makes a simple accompaniment for just about anything (made with a vegetable that never seems to go out of season).

Marinated Roasted Red Bell Peppers

Roast, peel, steam, and seed red bell peppers as directed on page 180. Leave whole. Sauté the peppers in olive oil with plenty of minced garlic until they are limp. Layer in a bowl and season with salt, freshly ground black pepper, and a drizzle of fine olive oil. (You may cut the oil with a few drops of lemon juice.) Serve at room temperature as an accompaniment to a roast or to plain grilled fish or chops. For an Andalusian touch, add cloves and bay leaves to the marinade.

SANDWICHES, BREADS, AND PIZZAS

Patafla

Here is one of the many rural recipes—like *tapénades* and country salads—that seem to have been invented independently all over the Mediterranean but are basically the same. The *patafla*, a kind of tomato and olive sandwich, differs from the similar Niçoise *pan bagna* only in that it has no anchovies. A good mixture of olives to use is a third crisp green, such as Sicilian style; a third marinated in vinegar, such as Kalamata; and a third mild ripe, such as Amfissa. The sandwich can be cut up and served as an hors d'oeuvre.

> **1 baguette, the crustier the better**
> **Fine olive oil**
> **3 tomatoes, peeled, seeded, and chopped**
> **½ purple onion, minced**
> **½ pound assorted brine-cured olives, pitted and chopped**
>   **(see note above)**
> **2 cloves garlic, minced**
> **½ red bell pepper, seeded and chopped**
> **2 tablespoons capers**
> **Salt**
> **Freshly ground black pepper**

Cut the baguette in half horizontally. Scoop out the moist center of the bread, break it into chunks, and place them in a bowl. Drizzle olive oil over the scooped-out bread halves. Add the tomatoes, onion, olives, garlic, bell pepper, and capers to the bread chunks and mix well. Add salt and pepper to taste, and enough olive oil to saturate the bread chunks thoroughly.

Fill one-half of the bread shell with the mixture. Cover with the other half and squeeze the halves together. Wrap well in plastic wrap and refrigerate for half a day.

Just before serving, remove from the refrigerator and cut into slices ½-inch thick. Arrange on a platter and serve.

Serves 4.

Bruschetta or Fettunta

Italian friends have reprimanded me for calling this bread-soaked-in-olive-oil *bruschetta*. If I use Tuscan olive oil, they tell me, it should be called *fettunta*. A friendlier chap tells me that the exact same dish is called a *tostada* in his part of Spain. I've no doubt that wherever there is a new pressing of olive oil, olive farmers and mill operators sample their oil in just this way, whatever their appellation for the treat. Remember it was conceived as a wintertime dish, to be eaten by the fireplace, although it can be made a seasonal dish any month of the year by topping with, say, melted Cantal cheese and pickled eggplant, red-ripe tomatoes and arugula (you can rub the tomatoes into the bread or leave them in slices), or steamed shellfish.

> **1 loaf crusty country-style white bread**
> **Garlic cloves, cut in half lengthwise**
> **A cruet of the latest pressing of fine olive oil**
> **Salt**
> **Freshly ground black pepper**

Cut the bread into slices ½ to ¾ inch thick. The traditional way to toast the bread is over a grill right in the fireplace; a charcoal fire in an outdoor grill will do the job just as well. Turn when the first side becomes golden brown. Toaster-broilers will toast the bread, but won't give the characteristic wood-fire taste.

When the bread is golden crisp on both sides, serve a piece to each guest along with 2 or more garlic clove halves. Each guest should then rub his toast with the garlic until it virtually disappears into the bread, drizzle olive oil over it until the toast is completely saturated, then sprinkle it with salt and pepper to taste. Serve with plenty of napkins.

Serves 12.

Muffaletta Sandwich

Some epicures and bon vivants would rather vacation in New Orleans than anywhere else in the world. New Orleans has its own cuisine and a long list of specialties, such as beignets, oysters Rockefeller, and, of course, muffaletta (the *e* is pronounced *o*, as in pot) sandwiches. Residents of New Orleans can't agree on which market makes the best; all the sandwiches are architectural accomplishments. There are similar sandwiches to be found around the Mediterranean such as *patafla* (see page 158), but none is so voluptuous and decadent, so exquisitely large, so pungent, so oily, so devilishly impossible to bite into, as an extravagantly made muffaletta.

For the olive salad:
  3 large cloves garlic, minced
  1 cup pimiento-stuffed green olives, chopped
  1 cup Kalamata olives, pitted and chopped
  1 red bell pepper, roasted, peeled, seeded, and cut into chunks (see page 180)
  1 cup fine olive oil
  3 tablespoons chopped fresh Italian parsley
  2 tablespoons white wine vinegar

1 large, round loaf country-style bread
1/3 pound or more salami, sliced
1/2 pound provolone, sliced
1/2 pound mild cheese (such as havarti), sliced
1/3 pound or more mortadella

The day before you want to serve the sandwich, prepare the olive salad. In a bowl mix together the garlic, olives, pepper, oil, parsley, and vinegar. Cover and let stand overnight.

To assemble the sandwich, cut the bread in half horizontally. Scoop out some of the center of the loaf and reserve for later use to make bread crumbs. Drizzle olive oil from the olive salad on both halves of the bread. The bread should be saturated. On one half layer, in the following order: salami, olive salad, provolone, mild cheese, and mortadella. Top with the other half of the loaf. Slice in wedges and serve with plenty of napkins.

Serves 6 hearty eaters.

Bread with Olives

This crusty bread from Tuscany called *pane con olive*, comes from a well-known Florentine cook, Giuliano Bugialli, who has added olives to a classic loaf. The addition of rosemary is mine. This *pane* is especially good with a hearty Italian soup such as minestrone (see page 106) or with a stew with a lot of gravy such as a beef daube (see page 124). Allow about six hours to prepare and cool.

For the sponge (first rising):
3 packages (scant 1 tablespoon each) active dry yeast
¼ cup lukewarm water
½ cup plus 1 tablespoon unbleached all-purpose flour

For the dough (second rising):
6 cups unbleached all-purpose flour
Pinch of salt
1¾ cups lukewarm water
1 teaspoon finely chopped fresh rosemary
2 teaspoons olive oil
½ pound Kalamata olives, pitted

To prepare the sponge, in a small bowl, dissolve the yeast in the water, stirring with a wooden spoon. Place the ½ cup flour in a larger bowl, add the dissolved yeast, and mix with a wooden spoon until all the flour is incorporated and a small ball of dough forms. Sprinkle the additional tablespoon of flour over the ball of dough, then cover the bowl with a cotton tea towel and put it in a warm place away from drafts. Let stand until the dough doubles in size, about 1 hour.

To prepare the dough, mound the 6 cups flour on a work board, then make a well in the center; it should have a large circumference and be shallow. Place the sponge from the first rising in the well. Add the salt, ½ cup of the lukewarm water, the rosemary and olive oil.

Using a wooden spoon, carefully mix together all the ingredients in the well. Then add the remaining 1¼ cups lukewarm water and start mixing with your hands, absorbing the flour from the inside rim of the well little by little. Keep mixing until all but 4 or 5 tablespoons of the flour are incorporated (about 15 minutes), then knead the dough with the palms of your hands, in a folding motion, until it is homogenous and smooth (about 20 minutes), incorporating the remaining flour, if necessary, to keep the dough from being sticky.

Add the olives to the dough and knead them until they are evenly distributed. Lightly oil a 10-inch springform pan. Place the dough in the pan, cover with a cotton tea towel, and put it in a warm place away from drafts. Let the dough stand until doubled in size, about 1 hour; the time will vary a bit, depending upon the weather.

Preheat an oven to 400°F.

When the dough is ready, remove the towel and immediately place the pan in the oven. Bake the bread until it is dark golden brown or until it sounds hollow when tapped, about 1 hour; do not open the oven for the first 30 minutes after you have placed the pan in the oven.

Remove the pan from the oven, allow to cool for 5 minutes, then release the pan sides and transfer the bread to a work surface. To cool the bread, stand it upright on one of its sides. The bread must cool for at least 3 hours before it is at its best for eating, and the room where the bread cools must be very airy.

Makes 1 loaf.

Pissaladière

This southern French version of pizza is quite a simple dish and is lovely as a first course. It is nothing more than an onion pizza, but the most common variations are topped with olives and are made, of course, with olive oil. The simpler the *pissaladière* is, the better. The black olive-anchovy version presented here can be modified by substituting bitter green olives and shrimp, or mushrooms and Niçoise olives. A hearty black olive, such as the Nyons, works best for this version.

> **1 package (scant 1 tablespoon) active dry yeast**
> **³/₄ cup hot tap water**
> **Olive oil, as needed**
> **2 cups unbleached all-purpose flour, or as needed for dough
>   and for dusting**
> **Salt**
> **Cornmeal for dusting, if needed**
> **2 yellow onions, thinly sliced**
> **3 tomatoes, peeled, seeded, and cut into chunks**
> **Salt**
> **Freshly ground black pepper**
> **8 anchovy fillets, rinsed**
> **²/₃ cup firm, flavorful black olives, pitted**

In a mixing bowl, dissolve the yeast in the hot water. Stir in 1 tablespoon olive oil. Add the 2 cups flour, little by little, stirring with a wooden spoon and incorporating a sprinkling of salt, until the dough is a workable consistency.

Turn out the dough onto a well-floured board and knead until smooth, about 15 minutes. You may have to add flour as you knead if the dough is sticky. Gather the dough into a ball. Oil a bowl, place the dough in it, and turn the dough to coat all sides. Cover the bowl with a cotton tea towel and allow the dough to rise in a warm place away from drafts until it doubles in size, about 1 hour.

In a skillet over medium heat, warm 2 tablespoons olive oil. Add the tomatoes and onions and sauté until the onions are soft and the liquid from the tomatoes evaporates, about 10 minutes. Season to taste with salt and pepper and stir to mix. Remove from the heat.

Preheat an oven to 450°F. If you have one, place a pizza stone 12 inches in diameter in the oven to preheat. Alternatively, lightly oil a baking sheet with olive oil.

On a floured board, using your fingertips or a rolling pin, pat or roll out the dough into a 12-inch round. Make a ½-inch lip around the edge of the dough. If using a pizza stone, slide the round onto a rimless baking sheet dusted with cornmeal. Alternatively, transfer the round to the prepared baking sheet. Scatter the onions and tomatoes evenly over the surface. Make an attractive grid pattern with the anchovies. Put the olives in the squares. Drizzle 2 or more tablespoons of olive oil over the pizza.

Slide the filled dough round onto the pizza stone or place the baking sheet in the oven. Bake until the crust is crisp and golden brown, about 30 minutes. Remove from the oven and brush the rim with olive oil. Cut into wedges and serve hot.

Makes one 12-inch pizza; serves 4.

Foccacia with Rosemary

There are two types of *focaccia* available in North Beach, the Italian neighborhood of San Francisco: a moist, springy *focaccia*, which is often topped with tomato sauce, and a lighter *focaccia*, sprinkled with herbs and made almost flaky by olive oil. A recipe for the latter follows. It must be served warm.

> **2 packages (scant 2 tablespoons) active dry yeast**
> **1 tablespoon sugar**
> **1 cup hot water**
> **¹/₃ cup olive oil, plus olive oil as needed**
> **2 teaspoons table salt**
> **²/₃ cup warm water**
> **5 ¹/₂ cups unbleached all-purpose flour, plus flour for dusting**
> **1 yellow onion**
> **Kosher salt**
> **Chopped fresh rosemary**

In a large bowl, combine the yeast, sugar, and the 1 cup hot water. Allow the mixture to stand until it bubbles and expands, about 10 minutes. Add the ¹/₃ cup olive oil, the table salt, and warm water, and stir to combine. Little by little, add the flour, stirring to incorporate it after each addition. The dough should be stiff. Turn the dough out onto a well-floured work surface and knead until smooth, about 10 minutes. Oil a bowl, place the dough in it, and turn the dough to coat all sides. Cover the bowl with a cotton tea towel and allow the dough to rise in a warm place away from drafts until it doubles in size, about 1 hour.

Meanwhile, slice the onion paper-thin and place it in a small bowl. Add water to cover and set aside.

When the dough has doubled, punch it down and turn it out onto a well-floured board. Using a rolling pin, roll out the dough to a size large enough to cover a baking sheet about 12 by 18 inches. Oil a baking sheet and transfer the dough to it. Cover with a cotton tea towel and let it rise in a warm place away from drafts until doubled in size, about 1 hour.

Meanwhile, preheat an oven to 400°F. Drain the onion slices and pat dry with paper towels.

When the dough is ready, "dimple" it all over with your fingertips, then dribble some olive oil evenly over the surface. Sprinkle with kosher salt, rosemary, and the onion rings.

Bake on the middle rack of the oven until golden brown, about 20 minutes. Remove from the oven and cut into rectangles. Serve hot.

Serves 4 as a first course.

Andalusian-Style French Toast

Dip bread slices in beaten egg and fry them in olive oil ½ inch deep over medium-high heat. Turn them once when they are golden brown. When the toasts have browned on both sides, remove them to a plate and add a few tablespoons of honey to the pan, adding more olive oil if none is left. Stir the mixture well, rub the toasts in it, turning to coat both sides, and serve.

Pizza Dough

A true Neapolitan pizza is quite different from the pizza most Americans know. It is baked on tile, not in a pan, in a hardwood-fired brick oven, and is topped with fresh tomatoes, not a thick, sweet sauce. The effect is a crispier, more breadlike dough and a more subtle product over all.

To approximate an Italian oven, buy enough quarry tiles (available at building-supply stores) to cover the middle shelf of your oven. The tiles must be heated at least 20 minutes at baking temperature (450°F) before they are warm enough to receive the pizza. Use a wooden pizza peel, a rimless baking sheet or the underside of a baking sheet dusted with corn-meal for transferring the pizza to the tiles. (The cornmeal will allow the pizza to slide off the paddle or baking sheet onto the tiles.) If you do not have a paddle or do not want to risk leaks, place the pizza in a cornmeal-dusted baking sheet on top of the tiles. You will miss the benefits of the absorbent tiles, which make for a crispier crust, but the extra heat will make the center cook at the same rate as the edges of the pizza. If you have no tiles, use an old, nonlaminated board, completely wrapped with aluminum foil and well oiled with olive oil.

The following recipe for dough can be used for any number of combinations of toppings, from salmon and crème fraîche to the one presented here, with cheese, anchovies, and tomatoes.

> ½ **package (scant ½ tablespoon) active dry yeast**
> ¾ **cup lukewarm water**
> 1½ **tablespoons fine olive oil, plus fine olive oil as needed**
> 1½ **cups all-purpose flour, plus flour for dusting**
> ½ **cup bread flour**
> ¾ **teaspoon salt**

In a large bowl, dissolve the yeast in the water and the 3 tablespoons oil. Allow the mixture to stand until it bubbles and expands, about 10 minutes. Slowly add both flours to the yeast mixture, stirring to incorporate after each addition. Once the elements are combined, turn the dough out onto a well-floured work surface and knead until smooth, about 15 minutes.

Oil a bowl, turn the dough out into it, turn the dough to coat all sides, and cover the bowl with plastic wrap. Refrigerate overnight, or let rise in a warm place away from drafts, until doubled in size, about 1 hour.

Punch down the dough and divide into 4 balls of equal size. Dust a work surface lightly with all-purpose flour. Using your fingertips, press one ball into a circle of even thickness about 7 inches in diameter. Pick up the circle between the palms and fingers of both hands and gently stretch the edge of the circle. Work around the edge, letting the dough hang. As the dough stretches to about 9 inches in diameter, drape it over the back of one hand and wrist and stretch it with the other hand. Continue working around the circle until the dough is about 11 inches in diameter, or, if you are using a rectangular baking sheet, 10 by 13 inches.

Once the dough is shaped, transfer it to an oiled foil-wrapped board or a cornmeal-dusted pizza peel or baking sheet (see recipe introduction). Pinch the edge of the dough slightly to form a raised rim. Top and bake as directed in individual recipes. Repeat with the remaining dough portions.

Makes enough dough for two 11-inch pizzas.

Neapolitan Pizza, Oliveto Style

At Oliveto, we offer about ten different pizzas on our menu. According to which one is being made, we vary the length of baking time (the more moisture and the more cheese, the longer the baking time). Our generic mix of cheeses is half Danish Fontina and half domestic handmade fresh mozzarella, both grated. Then we finish with a dusting of grated imported parmigiano-reggiano after the pizza is out of the oven.

> **1 recipe Pizza Dough (see page 167)**
> **12 tomatoes, peeled, seeded, chopped, and well drained**
> **8 cloves garlic, thinly sliced**
> **1 cup (about 4 ounces) grated whole-milk fresh mozzarella**
> **1 cup (about 4 ounces) grated Danish Fontina**
> **2 tablespoons capers**
> **12 anchovy fillets, rinsed (optional)**
> **Olive oil with an infusion of minced garlic**
> **Chopped fresh Italian parsley**
> **Hot-pepper flakes**
> **Freshly grated parmigiano-reggiano cheese**

Preheat an oven to 450°F (see introduction to dough recipe for directions on preparing baking surfaces). Shape the pizza dough as directed in the recipe. Distribute the tomatoes and garlic evenly over the surface. Mix together the mozzarella and Fontina cheese and strew evenly over the pizza. Top with capers and, if desired, anchovies.

Bake until the edges of the pizza are medium brown, about 25 minutes. Remove from the oven and brush the edges with garlic-infused olive oil. Sprinkle the pizza with parsley, hot-pepper flakes, and parmigiano-reggiano.

Makes two 11-inch pizzas.

DESSERTS

Chestnut Flour Cake

The recipe for this interesting Tuscan cake, called *il castagnaccio*, dates from the Middle Ages and the sweet is still much loved in pockets of the region. After serving the olive-oil-and-rosemary-flavored *castagnaccio* at a dinner party, I was told by a polite guest, "I like it because it's more resistible than the average dessert." I can't think of anything that would improve it, save using wheat instead of chestnut flour, eggs instead of milk, and so on. But then it wouldn't be *castagnaccio*.

It is a heavy, earthy-looking cake; you can count on most people not coming back for seconds. For tradition's sake, I include the recipe. Look for the chestnut flour in well-stocked Italian shops; seek out very fresh flour for the best results.

> **2 cups sifted chestnut flour, plus flour for dusting**
> **1 tablespoon sugar**
> **Pinch of salt**
> **3 tablespoons pine nuts, lightly toasted**
> **Scant 2 cups milk**
> **3 tablespoons olive oil, plus olive oil for oiling the pan**
> **1/3 cup raisins, plumped in milk**
> **1 teaspoon chopped fresh rosemary**

Preheat an oven to 425°F. In a mixing bowl, stir together the 2 cups chestnut flour, sugar, salt, and 2 tablespoons of the pine nuts. Slowly add the milk, stirring constantly so that lumps do not form. The batter will be quite fluid. Mix in 2 tablespoons of the olive oil. Drain the raisins and toss them with a little chestnut flour so that each is fully coated. Stir the raisins into the batter.

Oil a round, 9-inch cake or pie pan with olive oil. Pour in the batter. Sprinkle with the rosemary and the remaining 1 tablespoon each pine nuts and olive oil. Bake until the top is lightly browned, about 30 minutes. Remove from the oven and let rest on a rack for at least 10 minutes.

Serve hot or at room temperature, cut into wedges.

Serves 8 to 10.

Fruit Cake

Wonderful made with olive oil. A good combination is half butter and half olive oil. Make sure you use dried fruits with no artificial coloring, *toasted* nuts, and, if you've the nerve, a few green peppercorns.

Fritters Fried in Olive Oil

The dough for these fritters is nothing more than *chou* pastry, the same kind used in making éclairs and profiteroles. Here, however, the pastries are fried in olive oil and served plain, simply dusted with confectioner's sugar while still hot.

> ³/₄ **cup water**
> ¹/₄ **cup unsalted butter, cut into pieces**
> **1 teaspoon granulated sugar**
> **Scant 1 teaspoon grated lemon zest**
> **Pinch of salt**
> ³/₄ **cup all-purpose flour, sifted**
> **3 eggs**
> **Olive oil for frying**
> **Confectioner's sugar for topping**

In a saucepan over medium heat, combine the water, butter, granulated sugar, lemon zest, and salt. Heat, stirring, until the butter has just melted.

Remove from the heat. Add the flour all at once and, slowly at first, blend it in with a wooden spoon. Return the pan to medium-low heat and, stirring constantly, cook the flour paste for a few minutes until it comes away from the sides of the pan and gathers into a ball. Remove from the heat.

Make a well in the paste and add 1 of the eggs. Stir vigorously until it is thoroughly incorporated. Make another well. Add another egg and stir again until thoroughly incorporated. Repeat the process with the third egg.

Preheat an oven to 250°F. In a skillet over high heat, pour in olive oil to a depth of ¾ inch (even an omelet-size pan will do for frying about 4 puffs at a time). When the oil is hot, working in batches, spoon a generous dollop into the pan for each puff, keeping in mind that the puffs will expand to about twice their original size and must not run into one another. Keep the olive oil bubbling, being careful that it doesn't reach the smoking stage. Fry the puffs, turning once with a slotted spoon, until they are a rich brown, about 1¾ minutes on each side. Break open a puff to make sure the dough is cooked through. As each batch is cooked, using the slotted spoon, transfer to a plate with paper towels and put in the warm oven.

Arrange the fritters on a warmed serving platter. Sift plenty of confectioner's sugar over the top and serve immediately.

Makes about 20 fritters.

Citrus and Almond Cake

This cake, although heavy, is refreshing in its tartness. Be sure to use a flavorful olive oil—the fine, more delicate oils are overpowered by the citrus peels. It can be served with crème fraîche or lightly sweetened whipped cream, but it is also delicious without any adornment.

> 2 small navel oranges
> 1 lemon
> 6 ounces almonds, toasted
> Olive oil for oiling pan, plus ⅓ cup olive oil
> 4 eggs
> ½ teaspoon salt
> 1½ cups sugar
> 1 cup all-purpose flour
> 1 tablespoon baking powder

In a small saucepan, combine the oranges and lemon with water to cover. Bring to a simmer over medium heat and simmer, uncovered, for 30 minutes. Drain and let cool. Cut off the stem ends of the fruits and then cut the fruits in half; scoop out the pulp and seeds of the lemon and discard. Chop the oranges (with peel intact) and the lemon peel very fine. Place the chopped citrus in a sieve and press out as much liquid as possible. Set aside.

Preheat an oven to 350°F. Oil a 9-inch springform pan. Place the almonds in a food processor and chop until almost as fine as crumbs. Set aside.

In a bowl and using an electric mixer, beat together the eggs and salt until very thick and light. Gradually add the sugar while continuing to beat. Beat until fully incorporated.

In a small bowl stir together the flour and baking powder. Gradually, add to the egg mixture, stirring constantly; beat until blended. Mix in reserved citrus and nuts and the ⅓ cup olive oil; be careful not to overmix. Pour the batter into the prepared pan. Bake until a knife inserted into the center comes out clean, about 1 hour. Remove to a rack to cool. Release the sides from the pan and slide the cake onto a serving plate. Cut into wedges and serve at room temperature.

Serves 8.

Greek Walnut Cookies

In the Greek countryside these cookies, called *melomacarona*, are made by the kilo, and one of the ingredients is wood ash. This version is somewhat less earthy.

Some people prefer these cookies without a coating of honey syrup and walnuts, and I must say they are a more subtle treat prepared that way. Reduce the amount of ground walnuts to ½ cup if you plan on serving the cookies plain.

> ½ cup (¼ pound) unsalted butter, at room temperature
> ¼ cup olive oil, plus olive oil for oiling pan
> ¼ cup sugar
> 1 egg
> ½ teaspoon ground cinnamon
> 3 tablespoons freshly squeezed orange juice
> Finely grated zest of 1 orange
> 2¼ cups all-purpose flour, plus flour for work surface
> 1½ teaspoons baking powder
> Pinch of salt
> 1 cup finely ground walnuts, lightly toasted
> ½ cup honey
> 2 tablespoons water

Preheat an oven to 375°F.

In a bowl, beat the butter with a spoon until it is creamy. Add the ¼ cup olive oil and sugar and beat until fluffy. Add the egg, cinnamon, orange juice, and orange zest and stir well.

In a separate bowl, stir together the 2¼ cups flour, baking powder, and salt. Add the flour mixture to the butter mixture, a little at a time. At first the flour mixture can be stirred in, but when it thickens, turn it out onto a floured work surface and knead in the rest of the flour mixture. Then knead ½ cup of the walnuts into the dough.

Form the dough into a long roll about 1½ inches in diameter. Using the palm of your hand, flatten it slightly, then cut it crosswise into slices ¼-inch thick.

Lightly oil a baking sheet with olive oil. Arrange the oval-shaped cookies on the prepared baking sheet. Bake until the cookies are a delicate golden brown, 20 to 25 minutes.

In a small saucepan over low heat, combine the honey and water and heat the mixture until it forms a thin syrup. Spread the remaining walnuts on a dish. To serve the cookies, dip them in the syrup and then roll them in the walnuts.

Makes approximately 2 dozen cookies.

ABOUT THE INGREDIENTS

There are certain ingredients that one should always try to use in the kitchen: the best vinegars, seasonal produce, fresh spices and flavorings. In addition to those pantry items, here are some special ingredients—what we have found tastes best at Oliveto—plus a few basic methods.

ANCHOVIES. At Oliveto, we use only tinned, salted anchovies. They are far superior to oil-packed anchovies. Some delicatessens and specialty shops carry salted anchovies in bulk and sell them by the ounce for the home cook. Rinse the anchovies, then peel the fillets from the bone. If you do not use all the anchovies you buy, store the rest in olive oil in the refrigerator. The best are from Italy and Spain. Should you be unable to find the salted anchovies, use your favorite canned anchovies and run each fillet under hot water for a few seconds to remove the oil.

ARBORIO RICE. Because it retains its shape as it absorbs liquid, the best type of rice for making risotto comes from Italy's northern region of Piedmont. And the best Piedmont rice is rated *fino*. One needn't necessarily buy Arborio, for making risotto, but it is the most readily available of the Piedmontese *finos*.

BREAD CRUMBS. To make browned bread crumbs, shred stale white bread, omitting the crusts, and dry further in a 250°F oven, not allowing the bread to turn brown. Put the bread in a food processor and process until the crumbs are the right size. (You may store them at this stage in the freezer until needed.) Spread the crumbs evenly on a baking sheet and bake at 350°F until evenly light brown. Season appropriately.

BUTTER. This is an olive-oil book, so there aren't many recipes that call for butter. When they do, use unsalted butter. By the time salted butter reaches the consumer, more often than not it has been around for quite a while. Unsalted butter can be purchased by the pound and frozen in small quantities for everyday use.

CAPERS. The best capers available to us at Oliveto are salted capers from Sicily. We soak them briefly, then rinse off the salt. (For subtle dishes, rinse the capers a little longer.) They can be used whole or chopped in dishes. If salted capers are unavailable to you, use capers bottled in vinegar, preferably from Greece.

FETA CHEESE. This is a fairly soft sheep's milk cheese (or sometimes made from goat's milk) beloved by the Greeks. The United States imports feta not only from Greece, but also from Romania, Bulgaria, Israel, Hungary, Corsica, and Denmark. There is a domestic version as well. The Bulgarian feta is often the creamiest, but it is wise to ask your cheese merchants which varieties they like the best and why, then make up your own mind. Prices can vary considerably.

GARLIC. Most of us don't think of garlic as a seasonal crop because it is available "fresh" year-round. It *is* seasonal, however, and is at its best, and most mild, during late spring and through the summer (and even into fall). At other times it will have been in storage. During the off-season, remember to remove the bitter green sprout in the middle of each clove before using. That takes time, but is worth the effort.

HERBS. Many recipes call for dried herbs because fresh herbs are sometimes not available. The situation is rapidly improving, however; since the first edition of this book, all the most commonly used herbs have become available in well-populated areas year-round. As a general rule, fresh herbs may be substituted for dried herbs in the recipes in this book by more or less doubling the amount. Certain recipes call for fresh herbs and dried ones cannot be substituted. Basil, sage, and tarragon, for example, have a completely different character when dried. Dishes that call for these herbs should be served only when the herbs are available fresh. Oregano and thyme, on the other hand, are quite pleasant dried. Fortunately, herbs are easy to grow in window boxes, on decks, and in herb gardens, both indoor and outdoor. Many cooks insist that the best bay leaves are imported; I do like the flavor of the pungent California bay laurel in certain dishes, however.

HARD-COOKED EGGS. Start with the eggs at room temperature. Place them in a saucepan with just enough cold water to cover. The pan should be small enough for the eggs to fit snugly. Set the pan over a medium heat. Cover and allow the water to come to a boil. Take the pan off the heat immediately after the water boils and let it sit for seven to eight minutes, depending on the size of the eggs. Plunge the eggs into ice water. When they have cooled, peel them. They should be very soft, almost runny, in fact, in the very center; the yolk should be two-tone. Should you have newly laid eggs, keep in mind that a brand-new egg will be impossible to peel; let it sit for a few days before you cook it.

KOSHER SALT. The cooks at Oliveto come from diverse backgrounds and locations. They do, nevertheless, agree on salt: the best-tasting salt is kosher salt, the coarse salt that comes in an exotic box. When asked why it is better, they all say, "I don't know. It just tastes better." Use sea salt as an alternative, or just plain supermarket salt as a third choice.

OLIVES. In the recipes calling for olives, I designate the appropriate variety for the dish. If the variety is not available to you, refer to the Olive Glossary (pages 56 to 62) for olives that are similarly cured and therefore can be substituted.

OLIVE OIL. Recipes using olive oil call for either "fine olive oil" or "olive oil" (see pages 42 to 43, for information on purchasing oil). Fine olive oil is to be used as a condiment; cooking with it is a needless extravagance, since the flavors of the expensive oil are altered at high cooking temperatures. This oil should be your favorite cold-pressed oil, the oil with which you dress a salad or finish a chop, or serve at the table from a cruet. I have broken this category down further in my home: I have a very peppery, fruity oil I serve on rich or highly flavored dishes, and a slightly milder oil for salads made with delicate lettuces.

Olive oil refers to less expensive oil that need not have the attributes of a fine oil because it is used in cooking and will be altered by heating.

PARMIGIANO-REGGIANO. This wonderful aged cheese from Parma and its environs is well known and deservedly so. There is nothing like the authentic stuff–two to three years old and pampered from start to finish by the small producers who make it. So don't stint; get the real thing, for complementing your pastas, risottos, or salads.

ROASTING PEPPERS. Peppers that have beeen roasted have a wonderful smoky flavor. Evenly scorch the skins of bell peppers under the broiler or over an open gas flame. When cool enough to handle, rub off the skins, then remove the seeds. Leave whole or cut as directed in individual recipe.

SALADS AND SALAD DRESSINGS. The proper ratio of oil to vinegar for salads is as common a topic for discussion as the proper ratio of gin to vermouth for martinis. The exact proportions will depend on the tartness of the vinegar, the fruitiness of the oil, the bitterness of the greens, not to mention the tastes of the cook. But that being said, I believe there is nothing quite as honest or as delicious as a well-made, Tuscan-style salad, for which oil is measured in tablespoons and vinegar is measured in teaspoons–if any measuring is done at all. That perfect salad will consist of the freshest garden greens, the cook's favorite fine olive oil, a smattering of first-rate wine or balsamic vinegar to pour over them, and a little salt and freshly ground black pepper.

SUN-DRIED TOMATOES. A few recipes use sun-dried tomatoes, or *pumate*, available at specialty-food stores. Some are better than others, as you will see when you compare. They are quite expensive but a few go a long way. The delicious, sweet fruit comes packed in olive oil and will keep for weeks in your refrigerator.

TELLICHERRY PEPPERCORNS. Off southern India's shores lies the small island where these peppercorns grow. When compared to common peppercorns, they are far superior: they have a gentler pepperiness and a fuller flavor. If you've a specialty spice store nearby, by all means use Tellicherry pepper over any other.

TOMATOES. Although fresh tomatoes are available much of the year, freshly picked vine-ripened local tomatoes are available only a few months during the summer and fall. Canned tomatoes are far preferable to the mealy, pink, flavorless tomatoes in the market the rest of the year, or to fresh imports that may have been grown where the use of pesticides is even less well regulated than it is in the United States. Try the canned tomatoes that are available to you for the brand that tastes best. At Oliveto we favor a boxed tomato from Italy.

TOMATO PASTE. At Oliveto, we make our own tomato paste by reducing the liquid canned tomatoes are packed in, or, better, by collecting the tomato juice produced when one deseeds ripe fresh tomatoes and then reducing it in a heavy pan over a low heat.

THE BOTANICAL AND HORTICULTURAL OLIVE

It did not knock me for a loop
To learn the olive is a drupe.
So is the peach, or nectarine,
So is the purple plum,
and green.
But olives are the prototype,
The drupiest drupes,
both green and ripe.
So, like the botanist who knows
That the apple is a rose,
Just think,
"The olive is a drupe,"
When you put one in the soup.
—Marion D. Blyth

THE OLIVE HAS THE DUBIOUS DISTINCTION OF BEING THE original—the model—drupe. The Greek word *dryppa* and the Latin, *drupa*, mean overripe olive. Nowadays, drupe is the botanical designation for any fruit consisting of an outer skin (epicarp), a fleshy layer (mesocarp), and a hard and woody inner stone (endocarp), which encloses a single seed. The drupe group is a large and important bunch: cherries, prunes, plums, peaches, almonds, and apricots are all drupes. And berries, such as the blackberry and raspberry, are congregations of drupelets. I'll spare my readers the quadrupedantics of speculating on the true meaning of droop-eared (which is usually thus misspelled).

THE BOTANICAL OLIVE

In botanical nomenclature, plants are categorized first by family, then by genus, species, and, finally, by variety. The family to which our edible olive, *Olea europaea*, belongs is Oleaceae, of which the ash, jasmine, lilac, oleander, and privet are also members. Of the genus *Olea*, there are about thirty-five species, some of which are quite spectacular (like the *O. emarginata*, a large-flowered ornamental that attains heights of sixty feet in India) or exotic (like the *O. fragrans*, a small, odiferous species from China). None of the other olive species, however, bears an edible fruit. It is only the *O. europaea*, which has far too many varieties to count, that bears the fruit we press for oil and cure for eating.

The olive is a long-lived and tenacious—one might even say obstinate—plant, that grows in otherwise barren, sometimes arid, places on inhospitable soils of all types. It can live to be a thousand years old. Cut an olive tree down to its roots and from the earth many more will spring. In many localities it need not be irrigated or fertilized, although it is a grateful plant and repays kind treatment with bountiful crops. It does best in climates with long, hot summers, and requires a fair amount of winter chill for fruit set. For that reason it is not grown commercially nearer the equator than thirty degrees north or south latitude. Contrary to popular belief, it need not be near the ocean to thrive. (Nevertheless, Ernst McCormack swears he can hear the sea in an empty olive jar.)

The olive is an evergreen whose leaves are replaced every two or three years, leaf-fall usually occurring at the same time new growth appears in the spring. The olive's feather-shaped leaves grow opposite one another; their skin is rich in tannin, giving the mature leaf its gray-green appearance. Olive flowers are small and cream colored, growing on a long stem arising from the axils of the leaves. Because the olive is an evergreen whose leaves hide its flowers, olive-blossom time (usually in late spring or early summer) is not well publicized by the poets. The olive produces two kinds of flowers: a perfect flower, containing both male parts (stamens) and female parts (pistils), and a staminate flower, with stamens only.

Although most olive varieties are self-pollinating, fruit-set is usually improved by cross-pollination with other varieties. Honey bees are not necessary for cross-pollination if the different varieties are planted fairly closely, for the wind will carry pollen up to a hundred feet. There are self-incompatible varieties that do not set fruit without other varieties nearby, and there are varieties that are incompatible with certain other varieties. Incompatibility occurs for many reasons. For example, a certain variety of pollen on a certain variety of pistil might be adversely affected by high temperatures.

The olive has won a reputation as an alternate bearer, that is, bearing heavy crops one year, almost no fruit the next. That reputation is ill-deserved and, botanically speaking, untrue. When a very heavy crop is succeeded by a meager one, it is because the tree exhausted its resources so completely one year that it could not produce the next. The problem can invariably be avoided if the tree is pruned carefully every year. Pruning not only regulates production, but it can determine the shape of the tree to accommodate the method of harvesting or the tastes of the gardener. Peasants in Europe used to prune so that a natural ladder was created; multiple trunks can be created by letting either suckers or lower branches grow at the angle at which they are staked. The olive never bears fruit in the same place twice, and usually bears on the previous year's growth. Keeping these factors in mind, farmers can prune for consistent yields year after year.

The dimensions that an olive tree achieves depend on the variety, of course, but to an even greater degree on growing conditions. The largest trees grow in the warmest places, that is, in Tunisia, Morocco, and other North African countries. In California, the Tunisian variety, Barouni, grows no taller than its neighbors, be they Missions or Sevillanos, and comes twenty to thirty feet short of the height of its relatives in Africa, where there are some ninety-foot-tall specimens. Climate can so affect the growth habits of a tree that in some cases trees are difficult to identify by variety if they were propagated from cuttings brought from another climate.

It is for that reason the myriad olive varieties cannot be accurately counted; mankind has developed, preserved, and propagated innumerable bearing olive varieties. Some are disease resistant, some are cold resistant, some are drought resistant; some produce small olives with a high oil content, others produce ultra titanics containing little oil. Here are the exotic names of but a few of the major varieties grown in some of the commercial olive-producing countries of the world: in Spain, Manzanillo, Sevillano, Lechin, Gordal, Picual, Racimal, Argudell, Verdillo, Nevadillo blanco; in Portugal, Gallego, Verdeal, Cordovil, Carrasquenha, Redondil; in Italy, Frantoio, Moraiolo, Leccino, Agogia, Rosciolo, Raggia, Nicastrese, Biancolilla; in Greece, Caronaiki, Daphnoelia, Mouratolia, Carydolia, Stravolia; in France, Oliviére Pigalle, Pendoulier, Cailletier, Moiral, Picholine, Lucques; in Algeria, Chemlal, Adzeradj, Limli; in Turkey, Sam, Girit, Hurma; in Libya, Enduri, R'ghiani, Rasli; in Tunisia, Ouslati, Meski; in the United States, Ascolano, Sevillano, Mission, Manzanillo, Barouni.

olive lore:

Olive oil, olives, olive leaves, and olive branches appear in folklore throughout the Mediterranean as a means of guarding against everything from witches to overactive libidos.

Venetians say an olive branch on the chimney piece wards off lightning.

Throughout **Italy,** a branch over the door keeps out witches and wizards.

In **Spain,** an olive branch makes the husband faithful and the wife master of the house.

In Bilda, **Algeria,** there was an ancient olive tree into which the infirm drove nails to cure their ailments.

In **Lebanon,** during times of famine when only bread and oil were available, parents consoled their children by saying, "Eat bread with oil and hit your head on the wall." That means that such a diet will make you so strong you can take any kind of abuse.

warding off evils

In **Morocco,** to enter someone's house carrying olive oil and to leave without giving some away brings a curse.

In **Jordan,** the morning after a funeral and for the next three Thursdays (or Wednesdays, if the deceased was murdered) meals are served consisting mainly of various kinds of pancakes fried in olive oil.

In **Spain,** an olive tree touched by a prostitute or by an unfaithful husband will be unfruitful.

In **Portugal,** according to a legend connected to the Church of Nossa Senhora da Oliveira (Our Lady of the Olive Tree) at Guimaraes, the future king Wamba was herding cattle during the Gothic occupation at the spot where the Church now stands. Upon being told that he had been chosen king of the Goths, he thrust his staff into the ground and swore that he would not be king until that stick of olive wood grew leaves. God demonstrated his will by causing the stick to send forth not only leaves but branches and fruit, and Wamba agreed to be king.

THE HORTICULTURAL OLIVE

Most, if not all, the varieties of the species *O. europaea* were developed from the wild olive, or oleaster; consequently, none of the cultivated varieties can be propagated by seed. Seed-propagated trees revert to the original, small-fruited wild variety. Plants grown from seed must be grafted with plant material from the desired variety for the tree to have that variety's characteristics.

Researchers at the turn of the century were quite enthusiastic about grafting fruiting varieties onto rootstock produced from seed, the rootstock of such plants being robust, with a long tap root and symmetrical root system. Such a method of propagation proved to be tedious, however. Even after seed germination was hastened by cracking, or soaking in lye or sulfuric acid, plants grown from seed and grafted after two years seldom bore fruit before they were eight years of age. The method is not used as much today as it was a century ago.

A more commonly practiced method is propagation from cuttings: twelve- to fourteen-inch-long, one- to three-inch-wide cuttings from two-year-old wood of a mature tree are planted in a special rooting medium and kept moist. A tree grown from such cuttings need not be grafted to keep the qualities of the cultivated variety, although scientists are finding that combinations of certain varieties can retain the good qualities of both. Furthermore, a tree grown from a cutting bears fruit years before a seed-propagated tree, although not in large quantity.

A third method of propagation is transplanting suckers that grow at the base of mature trees. In most cases, however, those transplants have to be grafted because the suckers grew from the rootstock (and therefore the wild part) of the mature tree.

The variety of an olive tree can be changed by bark-grafting, or top-grafting. Most of the branches of a mature tree are cut off. Quarter- to half-inch-thick grafting wood (or scions) from mature trees of the new variety are wedged into the bark of the old tree where the branches were amputated. Usually there are three to four scions per stub. The wounds are covered with grafting wax to prevent infection by disease spores. The tree that has recently undergone this wretched operation is a sad thing to behold, but no, within three years, the new wood is bearing fruit and all is well for the next few centuries at least.

Experiments with olives are being conducted in all the olive-producing countries—by the United Nations, by national and state governments, and by individual farmers and horticulturists. Carlos Camacho, a Spanish olive grower, has been trying a new method at one of his farms: Every few years one trunk of each of his multiple-trunked trees is cut and grafted. Those multitrunked plants, then, are at once five, ten, and twenty years old. Thus, Camacho's orchards bear consistently year after year, never too young, never peaking, never declining.

The Food and Agriculture Organization of the United Nations with its network of olive-growing members is conducting studies with a number of the world's best-producing rootstocks, as well as with wild olive seedlings and seedlings of cultivated varieties. They use a system called "chip budding," where the grafting material is a small bud rather than a branch or twig.

Fertilizing olive trees with additional supplies of nitrogen has proved quite beneficial. In California, farmers systematically apply fertilizers well ahead of the time flowers develop so the trees can absorb the nitrogen before fruit-set. Some small farmers in the Mediterranean countries are less regular about fertilizing, applying organic fertilizers every couple of years. Other Mediterranean growers (like Maurizio Castelli in Tuscany, who fertilizes twice a year with both organic and commercial fertilizers) use scientifically determined regimes that produce the greatest harvests without damaging the trees or depleting the trees' resources.

In California, irrigation is a necessity because most of the olive orchards are situated where rainfall is unreliable, at best. In many Mediterranean countries, olives are not irrigated, even though harvests sometimes suffer during periods of drought. Because of its small leaves, with their protective cuticle and hairy undersurface that slows transpiration, the olive tree rarely dies during extended dry periods. Nevertheless, with the introduction of new agricultural methods, drip irrigation systems (some of them developed in Israel) are being installed by many Mediterranean olive growers.

Although the olive tree is affected by fewer parasites and diseases than most fruit trees, it does have natural enemies. Around the Mediterranean, the major pests are what we call the Mediterranean fruit fly, *Ceratitis capitata*, and the olive fruit fly, *Dacus oleae*. A fungal disease called peacock spot is a serious problem wherever olives are grown, affecting leaves and causing defoliation. An even more serious fungal disease for California growers is verticillium wilt, for which there is no effective treatment save avoiding planting on infested soils and removing damaged trees and branches. A bacterium

Van Gogh and the olive tree

Of all the painters who loved the olive tree, it was van Gogh who was most fascinated by the olive and who painted it most. And who could capture it better? He wrote from Provence: "I struggle to apprehend this. It is silver, perhaps a little blue, or perhaps somehow green-whitish bronze over reddish ochre earth. It is very difficult, very difficult. Even so, it attracts me. I like to contrast these colors with silver and gold. Someday I will obtain a personal impression as I did with sunflowers." He painted nineteen pictures of olive trees. *Olive Trees–Yellow Sky with Sun*; *Olive Trees–Bright Blue Sky*; *Olive Trees–Orange Sky*; *Olive Trees–Pink Sky*. How full of movement his silver-green trees are. Their elbows are gnarled, their roots are embedded in an undulating yellow earth, their leaves explode into the sky. The olive trees van Gogh painted when he was at the sanitarium in St. Remy are sad, seething monuments to his disturbed life. Those turbulent paintings notwithstanding, van Gogh did paint a happier scene with olives: a couple plucking olives from young trees in an *Olive Yard*.

causes a disease known as olive knot, which is spread by pruning with bacteria-infected tools during rainy months.

Because the olive has fewer natural enemies than other crops, and because the oil in olives retains the odor of chemical treatments, the olive is one of the least sprayed crops of modern agriculture.

GROWING YOUR OWN

I could think of no more beautiful tree to plant in my garden than an olive. So I bought one at my local suburban nursery from a nurseryman who could not let me take the tree home without relating the terrible story of how olive trees had ruined his life.

Many years ago, this lover of plants purchased a little house with an olive-lined drive. Over the next few years he tired of the purple-black stains on his driveway and chopped the trees down. They grew back, only now there were many times more of them. He chopped the trees down and dug out the roots over many months. The trees grew back. He chopped and dug, chopped and dug. And then, as a last resort, he poisoned. The trees grew back. He now has an olive-lined drive.

In this subdued man, however, there is a hint of awe and reverence—and even love—for those olive trees, in spite of the damage they did to his self-esteem. The trees ruined his self-image, but they demonstrated a dogged determination to be his companions. His story did not deter me. I have a little gray-green pal up on my clay hillside that I hope will, one day, have enough sunlight to produce enough olives to be fouling my footpath royally.

Here are some facts. Olives will grow well on almost any well-drained soil up to a pH of 8.5. They will withstand a very hot summer, but temperatures of lower than 15° F will kill the young olive. Olives require full sun. Winter chill is necessary for fruit-set, but lovely ornamentals can be grown where winters are mild.

The varieties commonly available in the United States are Sevillano, Ascolano, Barouni, Manzanillo, and Mission (with fruit size descending in that order). If you wish to have no crop, keep in mind that trees designated "nonfruiting" are not always barren; it is safer to prune fruiting wood each season. The Mission is higher in oil content than the other varieties, but home oil production is something to think twice about before trying. The Mission grows tall; the Manzanillo and Barouni have lower, more spreading growth habits. The Ascolano has a good flesh to pit ratio, and is resistant to olive knot. The Barouni, being a Tunisian variety, withstands extremely high temperatures.

If you plant a young tree, remove a few of the branches at the time of planting. The olive is slow-growing at first, but can be expected eventually to reach thirty feet in height and width in areas with hot summers and fertile soils. For a single trunk, prune suckers and any branches growing below the point where you want branching to begin. For the gnarled effect of several trunks, stake out basal suckers and lower branches at the desired angle.

Some farmers plant trees twenty feet apart, reap harvests until the trees are large, then, when the trees begin to encroach on one another, dig out every other tree, allowing the remaining trees to spread to full size. The trees that are removed do very well when transplanted. If you can find a source for them, you will have twenty years fewer to wait for a large tree. Whether it is young or mature, any newly transplanted tree should be watered frequently, but be careful not to overwater.

Olive trees can withstand radical pruning. Prune flowering branches in early summer if you wish to prevent olives from forming; fruiting can harm a lawn and discolor patios, decks, and walkways. Thin some interior growth to show the olive's branches to best advantage. Cultivate around the base of the tree to prevent competition with weeds.

Do not be impatient with your olive tree. It's an ill weed that groweth fast, and think of the pleasure it will give your great-grandchildren.

BIBLIOGRAPHY

Adams, Catherine F. *Nutritive Value of American Foods.* Agricultural Handbook No. 456. Washington, D.C.: USDA 1975.

Aguilar, Jeannette. *The Classic Cooking of Spain.* New York: Holt, Rinehart and Winston, 1966.

Antas, Mohamed A., Margaret Olson, and Robert E. Hodges. "Changes in Retail Market Food Supplies in the U.S. in the Last 70 Years in Relation to the Incidence of Coronary Heart Disease with Special Reference to the Dietary Carbohydrate and Essential Fatty Acids," *American Journal of Clinical Nutrition 14* (March, 1964).

Barich, Bill. "Tuscan Spring." *The New Yorker,* May 30, 1983.

Bates, Ralph. *The Olive Field.* New York: Washington Square Press, [1936] 1966.

Bensoussan, Meir, and Gabriel Grabi. "A Survey on Methods of Picking Olives for Pickling and for Oil." Tel-Aviv: Institute of Productivity, 1960.

Bergen, Lea. "Oil Fields," *Bay Food,* June, 1993.

Bugialli, Guiliano. *Classic Techniques of Italian Cooking.* New York: Simon and Schuster, 1982.

―― *The Fine Art of Italian Cooking.* New York: The New York Times Book Company, Inc., 1977.

California State Board of Horticulture. "Investigation Made by the State Board of Horticulture of the California Olive Industry." Sacramento: State Printing Department, 1900.

Center for Science and Public Interest. "Chemical Cuisine Chart." Washington, D.C., 1982.

Chimenti, Elisa. *Tales and Legends of Morocco.* Translated by Arnon Benamy. New York: Ivan Obolensky, 1965.

Ciurana, Jaume, and Llorenc Torrado. *Els Olis de Catalunya i la Seva Cuina.* Barcelona: Department d'Agricultura, 1981.

Consumer and Food Economics Institute. Composition of Foods: Fats and Oils. Agricultural Handbook No. 8-4. Washington, D.C.: U.S. Government Printing Office, 1979.

Coutance, A. *L'Olivier.* Edited by J. Rothschild. Paris, 1877.

Cronin, Isaac, Jay Harlow, and Paul Johnson. *The California Seafood Cookbook.* Berkeley: Aris Books, 1983.

David, Elizabeth. *A Book of Mediterranean Food.* Harmondsworth: Penguin Books, Inc, 1950.

——*French Provincial Cooking.* New York: Penguin Books, 1960.

Dean & DeLuca Imports, Incorporated. Newsletter. New York: Dean & DeLuca Imports Incorporated, March 1982.

Dinaburg, Kathy, and D'Ann Ausherman Akel. *Nutrition Survival Kit.* San Francisco: Panjandrum Press/MidPress Productions, 1976.

The Dispensatory of the U.S.A. 25th ed. Philadelphia: J. B. Lippincott Company, 1955.

Dobb, Edwin. "The Olive of La Falguera." *Discover,* May, 1991.

Donaldson, Dean, William A. Dost, and Richard Standiford. *Heating Your Home with Wood.* Agricultural Sciences Publications Leaflet 21336. Berkeley: University of California, 1983.

Edwards, I. E. S., C. J. Gadd, N. G. L. Hammond, and E. Sollberger. *The Cambridge Ancient History* 3rd ed. Cambridge: Cambridge University Press, 1975.

Fitch, Cleo Rickman. 1982. "The Lamps of Cosa," *Scientific American.* vol. 247, no. 6 (December).

Flamant, Adolphe. *A Practical Treatise on Olive Culture.* San Francisco: Louis Gregoire and Company, 1887.

Food and Agriculture Organization of the United Nations. *Report of the Third Session of the FAO Olive Production Committee,* Khania, Greece. Rome: F. A. O., 1976.

Friedman, Nancy. "A Short History of the California Olive." *San Francisco Magazine,* December, 1982.

Harris, Lloyd J. *The Book of Garlic.* Berkeley: Aris Books, [1974] 1979.

Hartmann, H. T., K. W. Opitz, and J. A. Beutel. *Olive Production in California.* Agricultural Sciences Publications Leaflet 2474. Berkeley: University of California, 1980.

Hazan, Marcella. *The Classic Italian Cook Book.* New York: Alfred A. Knopf, 1982.

——*More Classic Italian Cooking.* New York: Alfred A. Knopf, 1978.

Hilgard, E. W. and P. C. Remondino, eds. *Proceedings of the Olive Growers Convention, July 8, 1891.* Sacramento: California State Printing Office, 1891.

Hodgson, Moira. "A Sampling of the World's Olive Oil." *The New York Times,* September 2, 1981.

Huxley, Aldous. *The Olive Tree*. New York: Harper and Brothers Publishers, 1937.

Jacobson, Michael F. *Nutrition Scoreboard—Your Guide to Better Eating*. New York: Avon Books, 1975.

Johnstone, Mireille. *The Cuisine of the Sun*. New York: Random House, 1976.

Lelong, B. M. *The Olive in California*. Sacramento: State Board of Horticulture, 1889.

Luchetti, Fausto. "The International Olive Oil Trade." *Olivae*, February, 1993.

Majnoni, Francesco. *La Badia a Coltibuono—Storia di una proprieta*. Firenze: Francesco Papafava, 1981.

Marvin, Arthur Tappan. *The Olive—Its Culture in Theory and Practice*. San Francisco: Payot, Upham and Company, 1889.

Michaels, L. "Aetiology of Coronary Heart Disease: An Historical Approach," *British Heart Journal* 28, 1966.

Montagne, Prosper. *Larousse Gastronomique*. New York: Crown Publishers, Inc, 1961.

Morettini, Alessandro. *Olivicoltura*. Rome: Ramo Editoriale degli Agricoltori, 1950.

The New Encyclopaedia Britannica, Macropaedia, 15th ed. "Oils." Chicago: Helen Hemingway Benton, 1973-1974.

Nieto, J. Miguel Ortega. *Las Variedades de Olivo Cultivadas en Espana*. Madrid: Estacion de Olivicultura de Jaen, 1955.

Anonymous. "Oils and Vinegar," *The Gourmet Retailer* 4 (1983). No. Miami: Edward Loeb.

Olney, Richard. *Simple French Food*. New York: Atheneum, 1975.

Pect, Harry Thurston, ed. *Harper's Dictionary of Classical Literature and Antiquities*. New York: Cooper Square Publishers, Inc., 1965.

Pohndorff, F. *A Memoir on Olive Growing*. San Francisco: California State Horticultural Society, 1884.

Roberts, J. M. *History of the World*. New York: Alfred A. Knopf, 1976.

Root, Waverly. *The Cooking of Italy*. New York: Time-Life Books. Inc, 1968.

—— *The Food of Italy*. New York: Random House, Inc., 1971.

Shakespeare, William. *The Complete Works*. G. B. Harrison, ed. New York: Harcourt, Brace and Company, 1948.

Smith, William, William Wayte, and G. E. Marindin, eds. *A Dictionary of Greek and Roman Antiquities*. London: John Murray, 1901.

Standish, Robert. *The First of Trees–The Story of the Olive*. London: Phoenix House, 1961.

Sunset Magazine and Sunset Books, eds. *Sunset Western Garden Book*. Menlo Park: Lane Publishing Co., 1967.

Taylor, Frank. "California's Strangest Crop," *Saturday Evening Post*, October 2, 1954.

Waters, Alice. *The Chez Panisse Menu Cookbook*. New York: Random House, 1982.

"Why Greece's Coronary Rate is Low: Lots of Olive Oil?" *Medical World News*, March 15, 1982.

Wolfert, Paula. *Couscous and Other Good Food from Morocco*. New York: Harper and Row, Publishers, 1973.

York, George. *ABC's of Home-Cured, Green-Ripe Olives*. Agricultural Sciences Publications Leaflet 21131. Berkeley: University of California, 1979.

Zyw, Leslie. "Tuscan Cold Pressed Extra Virgin Olive Oil," *Petits Propos Culinaires 7*. London: Prospect Books, March, 1981.

TABLE OF EQUIVALENTS

The equivalents in the following tables have been rounded for convenience.

US/UK
oz = ounce
lb = pound
in = inch
ft = foot
tbl = tablespoon
fl oz = fluid ounce
qt = quart

Metric
g = gram
kg = kilogram
mm = millimeter
cm = centimeter
ml = milliliter
l = liter

Weights

US/UK	Metric
1 oz	30 g
2 oz	60 g
3 oz	90 g
4 oz (¼ lb)	125 g
5 oz (⅓ lb)	155 g
6 oz	185 g
7 oz	220 g
8 oz (½ lb)	250 g
10 oz	315 g
12 oz (¾ lb)	375 g
14 oz	440 g
16 oz (1 lb)	500 g
1½ lb	750 g
2 lb	1 kg
3 lb	1.5 kg

Length Measures

US	Metric
⅛ in	3 mm
¼ in	6 mm
½ in	12 mm
1 in	2.5 cm
2 in	5 cm
3 in	7.5 cm
4 in	10 cm
5 in	13 cm
6 in	15 cm
7 in	18 cm
8 in	20 cm
9 in	23 cm
10 in	25 cm
11 in	28 cm
12 in / 1 ft	30 cm

Oven Temperatures

Fahrenheit	Celsius	Gas
250	120	½
275	140	1
300	150	2
325	160	3
350	180	4
375	190	5
400	200	6
425	220	7
450	230	8
475	240	9
500	260	10

Liquids

US	Metric	UK
2 tbl	30 ml	1 fl oz
¼ cup	60 ml	2 fl oz
⅓ cup	80 ml	3 fl oz
½ cup	125 ml	4 fl oz
⅔ cup	160 ml	5 fl oz
¾ cup	180 ml	6 fl oz
1 cup	250 ml	8 fl oz
1½ cups	375 ml	12 fl oz
2 cups	500 ml	16 fl oz
4 cups / 1 qt	1 l	32 fl oz

INDEX